21229

THE MINISTER IN HIS STUDY

By

WILBUR M. SMITH

MOODY PRESS
CHICAGO

© 1973 by
The Moody Bible Institute
of Chicago

All rights reserved

Library of Congress Catalog Card Number: 73-7329

ISBN: 0-8024-5295-7

Contents

TO
my dear friend
and
fellow laborer in the word of truth,
Dr. Kenneth S. Kantzer,
Dean of the Faculty
of
Trinity Evangelical Divinity School,
whose vision and trusted leadership
in this decade
have made Trinity
one of the foremost
evangelical seminaries of the
Western world.

Preface

ON THE AFTERNOON of the last Saturday of May 1963, I had a telephone call from a person whom, as far as I know, I had not met up to that time. Dr. Kenneth S. Kantzer, for seventeen years, had been on the faculty of Wheaton College and, for six years, was chairman of the Division of Biblical Education. He had accepted an invitation to become dean of the faculty of Trinity Evangelical Divinity School, recently moved from Chicago to a seventy-nine-acre campus near Deerfield, Illinois in a location of great natural beauty.

Dr. Kantzer called to ask if there was any possibility of my becoming a member of the enlarged faculty which he was now planning. The amazing thing about this telephone call was that it was on that very day that my resignation from the Faculty of Fuller Theological Seminary was in the hands of my beloved friend, Dr. Charles E. Fuller. No one anywhere in North America knew anything of this resignation, except Mrs. Smith. Dr. Kantzer had no idea of such a move on my part. When I went out to visit the school, I discovered in Dr. Kantzer a man after my own heart; and it was not long before I firmly knew that here was one with whom I could joyfully work, one of those rare men of whom it can be said that "in him there is no guile."

I quote here from a letter that Dr. Kantzer wrote the following week: "I wish to state more clearly than I did in my earlier letter how much we feel your presence with us would mean for the Lord's work. . . . We feel that in this,

5

as well as in our premillennialism and in our puritanism, we are wholly one with you, and you would find yourself at one with us."

We had had our home in San Marino since 1947, and, of course, my library was being housed in adequate quarters in the library building of Fuller Theological Seminary. The arrangement entered into at this time was that I should teach the first semester of each year. In the fall of 1963, I went out to Trinity by myself. In the fall of 1964, Mrs. Smith and I lived in a mobile home provided on the campus; and in the following two years, we lived in one of the commodious apartments that had been erected on the campus.

The grounds and buildings of Trinity Evangelical Divinity School became for me, and will always remain, the most hallowed ground on the North American continent. From the very beginning, I was drawn to Trinity. Dr. Kantzer's own leadership and recognized gifts, the generous and open comradeship of the faculty, the enthusiasm of the student body, and that indefinable atmosphere of inspiration resting upon the institution formed a most perfect conclusion to the teaching years of my adult life. I shall always be grateful for the leading of the Spirit of God that allowed such a happy conclusion at that time of life. (I was sixty-nine years of age when the call came to go to Trinity.) The months spent at Trinity were for me "as the days of heaven upon the earth" (Deu 11:21).

When I went back to Trinity to give this series of lectures in the fall of 1972, I found the school possessing a greater faculty than ever and the largest hope-inspired student body that I have ever seen in a similar institution. I will never forget those mornings when I saw audiences every day of over four hundred people—students, faculty, and some visitors—so crowding into that lecture room that some found it necessary even to sit on the floor. One might speak of such an audience on the first day of the series of lectures as something to be expected, but how wonderfully gratifying it was to see that group every morning.

Unavoidable circumstances in the schedule of the speaker made it necessary to omit one lecture, which is included in this volume however—the one on the *Cambridge History of the Bible*. I trust that the lectures are not too heavily bibliographical. For each of the lectures, mimeographed outlines which included the names of the authors and titles of most of the books I would be recommending were distributed in order to save a great deal of toil in trying to keep up with the speaker in technical details.

These lectures are not to be considered as a survey of the best books for Bible study, which I attempted in the various editions of *Profitable Bible Study*.

I wish to thank the Cambridge University Press for their generous permission to quote extensively from their recent epochal *Cambridge History of the Bible*.

1

The Basic Books of a Pastor's Library

THE MOST IMPORTANT, frequently repeated event in the normal life of any minister, as the pastor of a church and a spokesman for God, is his message to a congregation of immortal souls, in that period of thirty minutes which falls somewhere between eleven and twelve o'clock each Lord's Day. That is the time when the Word of God through human lips should powerfully grip the minds and souls of men, leading to decisions and resolutions with consequences reaching into eternity. Our Lord Himself said of those of us who preach, "He that heareth you heareth me" (Lk 10:16). The apostle reechoed this in "Faith cometh by hearing" (Ro 10:17). This is when we hope that our listeners will, as the Thessalonians, "receive the message . . . not as the word of men, but as it is in truth, the word of God" (1 Th 2:13). What happens in that hallowed half hour will, apart from the anointing of the Holy Spirit, depend for the most part on the hours the minister has devoted to study and prayer in the preceding week.

It is these preceding hours of study I wish to discuss on the following pages. Morning after morning, alone in the study, the minister is confronted by the revelation we have in Holy Scripture. He seeks to comprehend something of the greatness of God, of the all-embracing salvation which we have in Christ, of the meaning of the church, of the

9

certainty of the life to come, of the destiny of the unbeliev-
ing, and of the life we ought to live until the Lord returns.

I will not discuss pastoral counseling, nor personal work,
nor evangelism, as important as these subjects are. I feel
there is no need to discuss *how* to study, for by the time a
man finishes seminary, his habits of study are generally
set. I am not going to discuss how to teach the Bible, nor
how to preach, though these are matters of the greatest
significance. In these pages my one theme will be, "The
Minister in His Study." First he must obey the Lord's
words, "Shut thy door" (Mt 6:6). I am assuming in this
book that, during the hours the minister spends in his
study, he will study. Too many ministers have changed
the sign on their door from the pastor's study to the minister's office.

Now any minister who is about to begin a lifelong study
of the Holy Scriptures and of the great literature that ex-
plores the profound themes of the Christian faith, must
make four preliminary basic decisions. First of all, he must
decide *how much time* he is going to give, every day, to
the study of the Scriptures and the great books of the
Christian faith. Let us often remind ourselves how rare
is this privilege of being allowed to determine what we
are going to do, or may do, those first three hours of the
day. We as ministers have a freedom of choice that few
have. Imagine a sergeant of the marines saying to a second lieutenant, "This is what *I* plan to do in the first three
hours each morning." Even a professor in a university or
seminary does not have such freedom as this, for he must
meet his classes certain hours every day or he soon will find
himself teaching the paternoster to sparrows on the limb
of a nearby tree. The pastor has the unusual privilege of
being allowed to plan his days according to his own de-
terminations and purpose in life.

The decision concerning the number of hours to be spent in the study is not the decision of what the minister *ought* to do, but what he is determined he *will* do. It is so easy to draw up beautiful plans, and chart exciting programs of study, but this is not the equivalent of studying. I am assuming that a serious-minded minister will set aside not less than three hours each morning, for five mornings a week of study. Let me encourage you regarding this matter of time with words from two gifted preachers of the twentieth century.

Speaking at Winona Lake in 1919, the greatest expositor of his generation, G. Campbell Morgan, confessed, "For thirty years I did not look at the newspaper until afternoon, for I had to work in my study, and did not want to contaminate my mind with worldly things when I had spiritual things to consider."[1]

And here are the famous words of one who during all his ministry had nothing but a crowded church before him, John Henry Jowett:

> If the study is a lounge the pulpit will be an impertinence. I remember in my earlier days how I used to hear the factory operatives passing my house on the way to the mills, where work began at six o'clock. I can recall the sound of their iron-clogs ringing through the street. The sound of the clogs fetched me out of bed and took me to my work. I no longer hear the Yorkshire clogs, but I can see and hear my businessmen as they start off early to earn their daily bread. And shall their minister be behind them in his quest of the Bread of Life?[2]

What great students and wide readers have been such preeminent preachers as Charles H. Spurgeon, H. P. Liddon, Alexander Whyte, Alexander Maclaren, and so many more! Any minister will find it difficult to maintain a study schedule of three hours each morning, but the battle can be won. Many duties and privileges and opportunities will come knocking at the pastor's study door to persuade him to leave that sacred place. And many of these are important in the minister's life; indeed some are unavoidable. Here is a list of common, tempting interruptions:

1. The normal work of the church: preparing for divine services, visiting members, planning funerals and weddings, writing the church bulletin (beware of spending too many hours on something that will be of no value the week after it is mimeographed), and attending committee meetings *ad infinitum*
2. The reading and answering of mail
3. Social engagements: activities with friends, group breakfasts which last until ten o'clock and ruin the morning, noontime speaking engagements with civic groups
4. The daily newspaper and the weekly magazines
5. Visitors (the wife should keep them away from the study in the morning)
6. Necessary shopping
7. A hobby or sport (no great preacher of the English world plays golf three times a week, as I know some ministers do)
8. Travel and holidays
9. Building operations, if the church is going through such an experience (a pastor should avoid better acquaintance with blueprints for a new auditorium than with the prophecies of Isaiah)
10. Denominational activities (shun consuming hours and days in these barren labors)
11. The family (this does not mean it belongs at the end of the list)
12. The telephone
13. That great demon, *laziness*.

All of these, some one day and some another, will try to allure him from his study, so that if yielded to, at the end of the day there has been no growth, no increase in the knowledge of God, no better understanding of His Holy Word.

The warning about time consumed in ecclesiastical entanglements uttered decades ago by Austin Phelps is more relevant today than when he wrote it, and I do not hesitate to repeat it here in full.

The best culture for success in the pastoral office is not consistent with the appropriation of any large proportion of time to the miscellanics of the church

I refer here to that department of clerical labor which is made up of executive affairs. A certain amount of this is necessary to the fellowship of the churches: therefore every pastor must so far supervise it. It would be dishonorable to shirk it. But, outside of the individual church and its immediate sisterhood, there is an amount of executive duty, which, as many practice it, becomes a profession by itself, to which the pulpit and its tributary studies are subordinated. The management of institutions, the direction of societies, the care of the denominational press, leadership in ecclesiastical assemblies, membership of innumerable committees, of boards of trust, of special commissions, all inflicting an endless amount of correspondence,—these form a distinct department of clerical labor, and create a distinct class of clerical workers. There are men, as you well know, whose chief usefulness is in this line of service. Their pulpits are secondary to it, and their libraries are more distant still from their chief ambition. If one of them were called to account for the neglect of his library, he could only plead, as did the ancient prophet of Judea, "Thy servant was busy here and there." , ,

Exceptions to the rule occur, as in the case of Dr. Chalmers, who, both as a preacher and as an executive,

was a genius. But such cases are not numerous enough
to affect the rule. Every young pastor, therefore, should
canvass and decide for himself the question whether his
mission of usefulness to the church lies in seeking or ac-
cepting any large amount of this kind of work. The in-
quiry should be answered early in his professional career.
I very well remember the form in which it presented itself to my own mind in my early manhood. I trust to the
freedom of the lecture-room in referring to it for the sake
of the glimpse it will give you of the opinions on the subject entertained by a considerable class of the older ministry. . . .

Will you be a committee-man, or will you be a preacher? Will you be a man of affairs, or will you be a scholar?
Will you be in demand as the ubiquitous delegate to
councils, or the executive leader of your presbytery, or
will you be a prince in your pulpit, with the accessories
of culture which that implies? Every pastor should decide the question with an enlightened policy, knowing
what he gives up, and why. Mediocrity, I admit, can be
gained in both departments of service. But ought any
young man to *plan* for mediocrity? The world is not suffering for the want of that commodity.

I think I have seen more deplorable waste of ministerial
force in needless dissipation of time upon executive mis-
cellanies than in any other form which has come under
my notice, which did not involve downright indolence.
. . .

Preach; let other men organize. Preach; let other men
raise funds, and look after denomination affairs. Preach;
let other men hunt up heresies, and do the theological
quibbling. Preach; let other men ferret out scandals, and
try clerical delinquents. Preach; let other men solve the
problems of perpetual motion of which church history is
full. Then make a straight path between your pulpit and
your study, on which the grass shall never grow. Build
your clerical influence up between those two abutments.[3]

It was said of the great R. W. Dale of Birmingham that "as he grew older he hardened his heart, and during the morning hours his study was obdurately closed against intrusion."[4]

The second decision a minister must make concerns the subjects he is going to study through the years, and how rich and inexhaustible these subjects are: cosmology, biblical theology, the New Testament world, the history of the ancient Near East, eschatology, Christology, missionary biography, contemporary philosophy of religion, the history of biblical versions and translations, the increasingly important subject of apologetics, the Qumran scrolls, and so forth. No one can be a master in all of these subjects; at least, not the average minister. Moreover, his interests will change from year to year. But there should be some definite plan in his mind as to the areas with which he hopes to be familiar. Who, for example, are the sixty contributors to the superb *New Bible Commentary* except men who began as pastors, probably of small churches, but by a determination to be good students ultimately became recognized as authorities on this subject or that. Some of you young readers will be writing the new Bible dictionaries and textbooks twenty years from now, and it will not be accomplished by those who spend more time before a TV than with the apostle Paul.

In the third place, after determining what subject or subjects he will be studying, the minister needs to decide *what books* he is going to read relating to that subject or subjects. This will be forever a crucial question for all serious students. He can't read them all, even in one major area. Take for example, the subject of eschatology. What an enormous literature has developed in this one fascinating area in the last thirty years! As an indication, A. L. Moore's *The Parousia in the New Testament* (Leiden,

1966), has a bibliography of 850 titles! And this is only *one aspect* of eschatology. It is in this matter of the choice of books that the normal minister will need guidance of one kind or another. Let me be very practical at this point. How is a young pastor going to know what *are* the best books written around some subject which he intends to investigate, or even the best commentaries on some New Testament book from which he plans to preach a series of sermons? Well, to begin with, there are some authors that immediately can be trusted, whose writings on *any* theme would be worthwhile (referring only to those now writing), such as F. F. Bruce, John Stott, Martyn Lloyd-Jones, Bruce Metzger, P. L. Packer, and Leon Morris. Then he will get help from book reviews, especially trustworthy help from the reviews in the principal evangelical journals, which I do not intend to list here. In fact, a minister would do well if having decided *what* he is going to study, he would spend a day in some large well-equipped theological library, where he can examine the major books of any given subject and can discover what he wants and what he doesn't need. This would be worth at any time a trip of two hundred or three hundred miles, or a day set apart in one's vacation. Then, of course, if he intends to do an exhaustive piece of work, he must consult the great *United States Catalogue,* though it contains no indication of the attitude of an author to the Christian faith.

After making three decisions (first, how many hours a week he will study; second, what subjects he will pursue; and third, what books on these subjects he will want to acquire and study), there is a fourth decision he must make: *how is he going to preserve for easy reference the material he reads on any theme?* This fourth decision is the subject that I will be discussing in the final chapter of this book.

THE VASTNESS OF THE MATERIAL

Before we begin referring to basic volumes for the minister's library, may I mention one matter that I hope will not prove in any way discouraging, and that is, the enormity of the material available today that relates directly to the interpretation of the Scriptures and Christian theology. Let me illustrate this.

In 1722 appeared the first good Bible dictionary of modern times by Augustine Calmet (1672-1757). This large five-volume folio work, *An Historical, Critical, Geographical, Chronological, and Etymological Dictionary of the Holy Bible,* was translated into English in 1732. In part 2 of volume 3 is an enormous bibliography of both Catholic and Protestant works relating to the Holy Scriptures—nearly 600 columns of bibliography, at least 12,000 titles, by 3,600 authors—important volumes that were available 250 years ago. It so happened that one of the outstanding New Testament scholars of our day, justly famous for his own published bibliographies, was in my study in 1971. When I showed him this volume of Calmet, he seemed stunned. He had never seen it before, and he knows the literature of biblical interpretation in five languages. When he got back to his own seminary where, of course, a copy of Calmet had been resting undisturbed for decades, he wrote, "I am reveling in the pages of Calmet."

To pass over the relevant bibliographies of 150 years, we come to the invaluable volume by John F. Hurst (1834-1903), *The Literature of Theology* (1895). This work lists about 5,300 titles, and the index indicates that 3,600 authors are here included, all in the English language. I have often expressed the hope that someone might be persuaded to give us a complete revised edition of Hurst, for thousands of important volumes on the interpretation of the Scriptures have appeared since the dawn of our century.

Let me mention one more quite exhaustive work, by the late Samuel G. Ayres (1865-1942), *Jesus Christ Our Lord, an English Bibliography of Christology* (1906). Here, arranged under sixty-four subject headings, are some 5,000 volumes devoted exclusively to the Lord Jesus Christ, all in English, and most of them, of course, of recent publication. This should also be brought up-to-date. If we add the 3,000 titles in Spurgeon's famous work to the lists of Calmet, Hurst, and Ayres we have in four works 25,000 volumes, allowing for 500 duplications, relating to the Christian faith *up to* the beginning of this century.

Because of the enormity of material relating to these subjects, and may I add, so much important material, it is so easy, almost unavoidable, for even the most serious-minded student to miss, to his own impoverishment, some truly epochal book, that has dropped out of sight during the last half century but is still of paramount importance. Let me illustrate this by an experience of mine of some twenty years ago.

I had as a guest for the day the president of one of the outstanding institutions for teaching the Bible in North America. He not only was its president, but every year, for fifteen years, he had been teaching a course in his institution on the epistle to the Romans. He really became excited when he discovered on my shelves a work that somehow he had never heard of, *The Explanatory Analysis of St. Paul's Epistle to the Romans* by H. P. Liddon. This work was begun in preparation for a series of lectures on Romans in 1876. It is based strictly on the Greek text and contains the most revealing and marvelously analytical outlines of this epistle that can be found in the English language. How much richer my friend's teaching of Romans would have been if he had been using this work of Liddon through the years. And such an oversight could so easily happen to any one of us.

I am hoping that what I have to say in these pages will still be worth consulting twenty years from now. I have tried to stay away from the literature of themes that are already retiring into the background, such as realized eschatology, demythologizing, form criticism, the nonsense of God is dead. I have felt it more worthwhile to commend a work that appeared even eighty years ago, such as Liddon's marvelous lectures, *The Divinity of Christ*, than a work of the 1970s on speaking with tongues.

Before we begin to discuss basic books and the literature of some great Christian themes, there is one question we must ask each man who, having finished his seminary training, is now beginning his first pastorate, and is about to set up a program for study—study which he must give to the preparation of his messages, and those additional hours of planned study which he should be giving to the great subjects of the Christian faith.

The question is this: what is the young pastor bringing into his study as he closes the door and is alone with God, with the Word of God, and with the book he is about to consult? What are the convictions he already has as he begins this time of study? The convictions which already possess him will have the geatest influence upon what books he will choose for reading, and what he will accept or reject.

Let me illustrate this. Some years ago I was doing some work in one of the best-equipped libraries of a theological seminary in the Middle West, when I observed one morning, as I came into the library, over 100 new copies of the work *Jesus*, by the French scholar, Charles Guignebert, translated into English in 1935. This was a volume in the

famous History of Civilization series. Guignebert for thirty
years was the professor of the History of Christianity at
the Sorbonne. In this book everything of a supernatural
nature in the gospels is repudiated—the virgin birth, the
miracles, the transfiguration, the resurrection, and, of
course, the deity of Christ, a strictly rationalistic work in
which the author says: "The truth is that we do not know
and in all probability the disciples knew no better where
the body of Jesus had been thrown after it had been removed from the cross, probably by the executioners. It is
more likely to have been cast into the pit for the executed
than laid in a new tomb."[5] We cannot help but wonder
how many students in that seminary using this volume as a
textbook came to *dis*believe in Christ as the Son of God as
set forth in the New Testament. Incidentally, the profes-
sorship that Guignebert held was filled upon his death by
Maurice Goguel, also a rationalist. One wonders how many
thousands of students, and scholars in France had their
own initial unbelief confirmed in the reading of such a
work as Guignebert? There are hundreds of ministers in
our country, Guignebert or no Guignebert, who have come
to this tragic conclusion. Most of them will avoid reading
conservative literature. What such men need is a reconsid-
eration of the historic certainities of these great events in
our Lord's life, and this takes us into Christian apologetics.
But apologetics is a vast subject of its own, and I will not
be dwelling upon it in this book.

In the preparation of these chapters, I had in mind believing clergymen, those whose faith in the veracity of the
New Testament is unshakable. I can only speak out of
my own conservative position toward the Christian faith
and the Scriptures.

Let me repeat: much that will happen in the pastor's
study will be determined by what he brings into the study

as he commences his ministry, though we might well hope that some who begin their pastorate in unbelief might be persuaded to read some great work in the defense of the faith, or the life of our Lord which would change their own convictions from unbelief to deep belief in the divine origin of the Holy Scriptures.

BASIC BOOKS

In these pages I want to be of some help in guiding you through the all-important and ever-multiplying literature of our glorious faith. Before I suggest specific books for your library, however, may 1 emphatically affirm that in all your hours in the study the Holy Scripture must be first and central.

One of the most important decisions which any serious student of the Word of God must make pertains to the version or versions with which he intends to work. There is great uncertainty today about versions. One man quotes from one version, and another from another. There is a danger that instead of carefully studying the text of one dependable version, we flit from one to another until confusion follows. Personally, I believe that the English text today which is nearest to the Hebrew and Greek versions is *The New American Standard Bible* which is based upon that great American Standard Version of 1901. The New Testament section appeared in 1960 and the entire Bible in 1971, the result of years of labor by some of the outstanding conservative Bible scholars of our day.

THE OCTAPLA

One of the most helpful books for the study of the various important versions of the English Bible is the large quarto *New Testament Octapla*, edited by Luther A. Weigle of Yale, and published by Thomas Nelson and Sons.

Here we have the principal eight versions of the English
Bible printed in parallel columns beginning with the Tyn-
dale version of 1525 and terminating with the Revised
Standard Version of 1960.

Whatever a minister's eschatological views might be, he
would do well to have near at hand the *New Scofield Reference Bible*, which appeared in 1967, after ten years of
work. Some of the notes in this Bible are the most helpful
that are to be found in any reference Bible in the English
language. For example, that marvelous page (913) on the
seventy weeks of Daniel is the most helpful note of its size
that I have ever seen on this difficult but important passage. Speaking of versions, one will find much information
in the following volumes: *The Bible in Its Ancient and
English Versions*, edited by H. Wheeler Robinson and published by the Oxford University Press in 1940; *The English
Bible, a History of Translations*, by F. F. Bruce and also
published by the Oxford Press, in 1961 (revised edition,
1970); and a briefer work, *A Guide to Modern Versions of
the New Testament*, by Herbert Dennett and published by
Moody Press.

The student of the New Testament is wonderfully provided today with lexicons of the Greek New Testament far
superior to anything that has hitherto been known. The
best one-volume lexicon is, of course, *a Greek-English
Lexicon of the New Testament and Other Early Christian
Literature* by Walter Bauer, translated and edited by William F. Arndt and F. Wilbur Gingrich, and published by
the University of Chicago in 1957. Here we have what
most earlier lexicons did not attempt—marvelous bibliographies of relevant books and articles in English and
the Continental languages. Even in a great work like this,
however, there are disappointments, for example the amazingly worthless statement regarding *theopneustos* (2 Ti

3:16), with no hint of the great discussion of this rare word by B. B. Warfield in his epochal volume, *Revelation and Inspiration.*[6]

Then, of course, there is this monumental *Theological Dictionary of the New Testament*, which first appeared under the editorship of Gerhard Kittel, and, beginning with volume 5, by Gerhard Friedrich. Thus far, eight volumes have appeared—one more is yet to come—7,758 pages on the words of the Greek New Testament. Some articles that are equivalent to an entire book, as for instance, the more than 120 pages on the one word *pneuma*. Geoffrey Bromiley has done a marvelous piece of work in translating these volumes, one by one, nearly 8,000 pages in less than ten years! Of course, the Kittel work is the result of the labors of scores of New Testament scholars. There are some weaknesses, as all admit, but it will remain for generations as an indispensable tool for the study of the Greek New Testament. Most of us could wish, however, that it had been possible to add some titles exploring the meaning of these words that have appeared in the English language. Bromiley has not felt at liberty to make such additions.

ATLASES

The British firm of Thomas Nelson has, during the last twelve years, published four great atlases that would be of greatest help to any serious student of the Scriptures and biblical times. All these volumes are of the same size, 10½ by 14¼ inches. First there appeared the *Atlas of the Early Christian World* (1958) with maps locating all the early churches, monasteries, centers of learning, et cetera. In the following year appeared the great *Atlas of the Classical World* with 70 maps and 470 illustrations. In 1962 appeared the *Atlas of Mesopotamia*.

The most important of all for our purpose, however, is the *Atlas of the Bible*, by L. H. Gröllenberg, translated from the earlier Dutch edition by J. M. H. Reid and H. H. Rowley, published in 1956 with 408 illustrations and 36 maps. One cannot speak too highly of this work.

Gröllenberg is a member of the Paulist Order, but his work exhibits no particular slant toward Catholic tradition. In fact, he goes so far as to refrain from publishing any pictures of the Church of the Holy Sepulchre, because, he says, the present structure is so unlike anything originally erected there.

The index itself is almost a Bible dictionary, and justifies the opening statement: "The principal purpose of this index is to catalog and describe all the *geographical indications* provided by the Bible. It therefore contains the name of every town and village, every mountain and valley, and every region, river, country, and people which occurs in the Bible."[7]

On the final page, Gröllenberg himself makes this statement:

> The Christian of today shares the views of the Early Church. He knows that he is living in the latter days, in the closing phase of world history. Whether this period be long or short, all that now matters to each man is to find God in Christ. Henceforward it is impossible to propose any other way of salvation in the name of God. In Jesus He has said all and given all. Even God cannot give more than Himself. For all Christians the Bible shares the definitive character of the historic revelation of God in Jesus Christ. Like that revelation, it can never be replaced or surpassed.[8]

Let me here call attention to a volume that I have discovered is not well-known even among professors in theological seminaries. This is an *Atlas of the Life of Christ*, edited by the late John Stirling, of the British and Foreign Bible Society, and published, now in its fourth edition, by George Philip and Son of London, a small volume, 5½ by 8½ inches, that can easily be put in one's pocket. The cartography is the very best. Of the forty-four maps, nineteen relate to the life of Christ, one showing the important sites of His birth and childhood, another indicating His residence in Nazareth and early visits to Jerusalem, and a most interesting one, different from anything I have ever seen, a map of the distances from various cities in Palestine given in miles and kilometers. In addition to the numerous maps relating to Paul's great ministry, there are separate maps on the missions of Philip, Peter, and Barnabas. One of the most valuable factors in this atlas is the list of Christians living in any one city, for example, on the map of Paul's companions during his sojourn at Ephesus 54-56 A.D. there are twenty Christians listed (with references) as living in Ephesus, and five more who "later turned from the faith." I cannot recommend this atlas too highly.

BIBLE DICTIONARIES

My own opinion is that many ministers, indeed the majority of ministers, rob themselves of much rich material relating to their studies that is to be found in Bible dictionaries. The truth is that there are many articles in the more important Bible dictionaries on certain subjects that are more informing than many books on the same subject might be.

The greatest of all Bible dictionaries of the later nineteenth century was the one edited by William Smith, the *Dictionary of the Bible*, first appearing in 1863 in four volumes, put together with the help of sixty of the outstanding biblical scholars of that time, including such men as Dean Alford, Bishop Ellicott, Lord Hervey, the famous botanist Joseph D. Hooker, Principal Howson (of the Conybeare and Howson *Life of St. Paul*), J. B. Lightfoot, the Perownes, Reginald S. Poole of the British Museum, George Rawlinson (the distinguished professor of English History at Oxford), Dean Stanley, Samuel Tregelles, Henry Tistram (the best authority on Palestine in his day), Canon Wordsworth, and the inimitable Bishop Westcott. What a galaxy of scholars!

While the discussions on archaeology and some historical subjects are now outdated, still there are many articles here well worth reading, for example, the thirty columns on David. In the middle of the first volume is an elaborate series of articles relating to the church. After some sixteen columns of text on the "Church," one comes upon *five columns of bibliography* on this one subject, in its various aspects: "Church in General," "Church and the State," "History of the Eastern Churches," "History of the Reformation," "History of the Church of England," and "Other Branches of the Church in England and America." These five columns contain the most important bibliography of the Christian church I have seen in any dictionary in the English language.

While we are discussing Smith's great dictionary, we should not forget that in 1887, the editor, in cooperation with Dean Henry Wace, gave to the world the last of his famous dictionaries, *A Dictionary of Christian Biography, Literature, Sects and Doctrines*, a four-volume work covering every important name in the history of the Christian church down to the eighth century; superior, I would say, to any other dictionary of this period in any language. Many of the longer articles were written by the greatest biblical scholars of the latter part of the nineteenth century—such as Hort, Westcott, and Lightfoot. In some of our more popular magazines today we occasionally see sensational announcements of some work entitled, "The Lost Books of the Bible," or "The Book of Adam and Eve," but eighty years ago the famous classical scholar, F. J. Hort, wrote an article of ten columns for this work entitled, "The Book of Adam."

In the first volume are magnificent discussions of "Angels," "Antichrist," the apologist "Athanasius" (25,000 words), even a ten-column article on "Attila the Hun." The section on "Basilides," the founder of gnosticism in the second century extends to thirteen pages, and that on "Basil," bishop of Caesarea, to fifteen pages. The 28,000 words on "Judah and Judaism" could well constitute a separate book on the subjects. Here we find exhaustive discussions of "Chrysostom," "Clement of Alexandria," "Constantine" (fifty columns), the "Coptic Church," "Cyril of Jerusalem" (fourteen pages), "Donatism" (thirty-two columns), "Demonology," the "*Chronicon Paschal,*" et cetera. There has been no great addition to our knowledge of most of these subjects since these volumes were published. They offer an education in church history to anyone who will shut the door and soberly study these pages.

The most important series of Bible dictionaries ever to be edited by one man are the ten volumes done by James Hastings, which consist of the five-volume *Dictionary of the Bible* (1905-9); the single volume, a condensation of the earlier work, *A Dictionary of the Bible* (1909); *A Dictionary of the Apostolic Church,* (1916-18), two volumes; but above all, the *Dictionary of Christ and the Gospels* (1908), two volumes. I think if I had the choice of just two volumes out of any set of Bible dictionaries published in the last century, I would choose these two volumes relating to Christ and the gospels. The work has been done so thoroughly that there are seventy different articles, some brief and some long, bearing upon the sub-

ject of our Lord's nativity. It has often been said, and
truthfully so, that the single article, "Character of Christ,"
by T. B. Kirkpatrick, extending to thirty-four columns of
text, is the finest discussion of this subject that has appeared this century. An unexpected contribution in defense
of conservative Chistology is the article, "Fact and The-
ory," by C. W. Hodge of Princeton Theological Seminary.
Here and there one will be surprised at what he discovers,
as for instance, eight columns on the subject of children,
by Warfield, which contains the best treatment of Mark
10:14-15 that one will find in any available literature. The
article, "The Divinity of Christ," extends to thirty columns
and is worth reading once every year.

Then one should not have far from his desk the still important *International Standard Bible Encyclopaedia* (ISBE)
first published in 1915, but thoroughly revised for the five-
volume edition of 1930. I well remember the day when
J. Gresham Machen was visiting in my home in Coatesville
and was looking over my then quite modest library. When
his eye fell upon this work, he took volume one from the
shelf, and opening it to the article, "Chronology of the
New Testament," by his colleague, William P. Armstrong,
of Princeton, he asked me the embarrassing question,
"Have you mastered this article?" And I had to confess
that I had not. He caressed the page and said, "This is a
precious work, and you should give it careful study." I
recall another incident relating to this work when I was
visiting in the home of my dear friend D. J. DePree in
Zeeland, Michigan, a constant student of the Scriptures,
and a layman quite gifted in teaching the Word of God,
himself possessing an excellent library of biblical literature.
While we were talking, he asked me if I knew anything
that would help him in the study of the genealogies of the
Scriptures. I told him, of course, there was really a great

article in the *International Standard Bible Encyclopaedia*. This he had never heard of, so we immediately drove into Grand Rapids to Kregel's bookstore and found an unused set in perfect condition. There was the article, twenty-four columns long (vol 2, pp. 1183-96), by one whose name is now wholly forgotten. It must have cost him two years of work at least. I am quite sure that the subject index of this Bible dictionary or biblical encyclopedia is the most exhaustive index of its kind, where appear over 23,000 subjects.

The one-volume *Dictionary of the Bible* which was edited by Hastings in 1909, considered by many even more important than the five-volume *Dictionary of the Bible* edited by Hastings, appeared in a revised edition, a volume of 1,060 pages, of double column pages edited by F. C. Grant and H. H. Rowley. Some articles are exactly the same as in the earlier edition. Others have been partly modified. Some have been wholly rewritten, and some are new. For the first edition, Hastings had the help of 106 scholars. For the new edition 160 scholars contributed including 73 from America. Here one will find an article on Jesus Christ of thirty-two columns and on christology of twenty-six additional columns.

RECENT BIBLE DICTIONARIES

The matter of Bible dictionaries is liable to prove somewhat confusing just now. Actually in the ten year period, from 1960-1970, twenty-six different Bible dictionaries appeared in the English language. Some of these were reprints, as the great twelve-volume work of McClintock and Strong, and a new edition of the famous Smith's *Dictionary of the Bible*. Two dictionaries appeared in revised editions—the one-volume work edited by Hastings and the *New Westminster Bible Dictionary* edited by Gehman.

Unger's *Bible Dictionary* appeared in the third edition,
and *Harper's Bible Dictionary* in the seventh edition. Then,
of course, there were dictionaries entirely new, such as the
great Inter-Varsity *New Bible Dictionary* and the four-
volume *Interpreter's Bible Dictionary;* but some of these
works were trivial and need not even be specifically referred
to. Some were small and some were large, some were cheap
and some are expensive, including two that are listed at
$17.50. H. H. Rowley, one of the greatest scholars of our
generation, took advantage of this interest in Bible dictionaries by issuing three volumes within a period of three
years, *Dictionary of Bible Themes*, 1968; *A Short Dictionary of the Bible*, 1968; and *A Dictionary of Bible Place
Names* in 1970.

An indispensable work was published by Inter-Varsity
in 1962, *The New Bible Dictionary*, the efforts of twenty-
nine different scholars. The great charts of Donald Wiseman, then of the British Museum, now a professor at the
University of London, is easily worth the price of the book.
Here one will find a chart listing all the excavations in the
Mesopotamian Valley and in Palestine and Syria giving
the dates of the principal excavations, the principal results,
the organizations carrying on these projects and references
to the literature where these matters are discussed. Wiseman himself wrote seventy-five of the short articles and
twenty-four of the long articles including a great contribution, "Writing," twenty columns long. Sometimes the contemporary enthusiasm for archaeology results in a dispro-
portion of space, some of us would think. Thus, thirty
columns are devoted to Egypt but only twenty-five columns to the apostle Paul. Nebuchadnezzar receives two
columns, while cosmetics and perfumery receive four and
eight columns respectively. The bibliography on the apostle Paul is the best of any Bible dictionary that we have.

Archaeology, including the great chart of fifty-three arch-aeological excavations receives thirty-one columns and Babylon with a chart of twenty-four excavated sites receives nineteen. What tremendous things have been dis-cussed in the area of archaeology in the last half century, Megiddo (1925-39); Nuzi (1925-31); Ras Shamra (Ugarit) (1928); the Lachish Letters (1932-38); Qumran (1948-58); Neolithic Jericho (1952-58); and lately the explora-tions of Jerusalem.

In 1964 there was published at Tel Aviv and by Macmil-lan in New York, a very interesting volume, *The Pictorial Biblical Encyclopedia*, with the subtitle, *A Visual Guide to the Old and New Testaments*, a large quarto work of over 700 pages with 813 illustrations. In archaeological matters and those that pertain to the Old Testament, the book has some very excellent articles. But it is interesting—as it was supposed to embrace New Testament subjects—that there are no articles here on the cross, the crucifixion, the virgin Mary, et cetera. There is, however, a very remark-able article on Jesus Christ in which the following tribute is paid to Jesus.

> The message of Jesus rising from the dead, apparently came as a shock to the early disciples who were still look-ing for a "royal" messiah and lacked the necessary con-ception of Jesus as a suffering messiah, for which his death and resurrection were essential.

> From a modern, naturalistic view of history, the death resurrection of Jesus remains a mystery, which can only be solved in terms of a philosophical or religious creed. Perhaps the best that can be said scientifically is that if Jesus was the kind of person who could inspire the con-viction that his death/resurrection was a necessity, then this, in itself, was a miracle humbly accepted by the faithful. Through its mystic aspects, it has immeasurably enriched the spiritual and philosophical life of the world.[9]

is brief, the article "BLESS" is something that every minister will find most helpful, a word so frequent in the Scriptures and yet so rarely discussed.

A volume that was published by the Oxford University Press in 1958 did not get the attention that it deserves. This is *A Companion to the Bible* edited by J. J. Von Allmen of the University of Neuchatel. He has received the help of thirteen continental scholars in preparing the original French edition of 1954, of which this is a translation. "The task we have set ourselves is to present to the wider public an exact realization of the full and rich significance which our words assume when they are chosen to be the vehicles of the Word of God."[10]

Of the many theological dictionaries available, one of the best is Baker's *Dictionary of Theology* edited by Everett Harrison, published in 1960. Here are some articles that one normally would not find in such a work as Wooley's "School of Alexandria"; Bruce on the Dead Sea scrolls; a helpful article "The Fate of the Heathen," and four different articles on baptism by Bromiley.

Of Roman Catholic origin, there is the *Dictionary of Theology* edited by Ernst Cornelius (Herder & Herder, 1965) with long articles on creation, faith, penance, and the anointing of the sick.

Here again are articles on some subjects that one does not commonly find in works of this kind, for example, an article of 3,500 words on *inheritance*, an article of 3,000 words on *clean*, ten columns on the simple, but important word, *call*, and ten columns on the subject that is now getting so much attention, *death*. A word of great frequency in the New Testament, but difficult to define, is *glory*, to which an article of 3,000 words is assigned.

James Pritchard of the University of Pennsylvania edited an amazing work, *The Ancient Near Eastern Texts*.

Here is brought together translations of almost all the literature of the ancient Near East that has any bearing upon the Scriptures of the Old and New Testaments. The translations have been done by leading Orientalists and carry excellent bibliographies. The second edition, with considerable additions, including material from Qumran was published in 1955. A corollary work also edited in 1954 by Pritchard, *The Ancient Near East in Pictures Relating to the Old Testament*, is a collection of over 750 pictures arranged according to subjects.

One other work in the area of archaeology should be mentioned here, and that is *Light from the Ancient Past* by Jack Finegan, published by Princeton University Press. A second edition appeared in 1959. This contains a discussion of almost all the archaeological discoveries of this century as they relate to the Old and New Testaments with superb illustrations and very adequate references to the relevant literature. Finegan recently has published *The Archaeology of the New Testament*, also published by Princeton, but it is quite expensive ($20).

While we are speaking about archaeological matters, may I call attention to a work rarely seen anywhere in this country published in Jerusalem in 1954 with the title *Jerusalem the Saga of the Holy City*. This magnificent work of 12½ by 13½ inches, in addition to an extensive textual introduction and an extensive bibliography, includes twenty-three maps, some of them folding maps inserted in the inside of the back cover. These include drawings of what the city may have looked like under the Jebusites, the city of the first temple, the acropolis of King Solomon, and the maps of the city in various epochs down to "A Bird's-eye View of the Holy City" in 1947. Attached to some of these maps are lists of identified places, sometimes exceeding 100 locations on a single map.

At the end of this chapter, I now move away from these technical matters and bring to your heart and mind these words of that great saint, hymnwriter, and man of God, Andrew Bonar. He wrote in his famous, heartmoving diary, "Led today to notice that all my books that come to help my study and suggest what I might preach, as well as those papers, and the like, that stir up the soul, are all part of God's calling of me. By these He carries on what He began, and so by every verse of Scripture which He gives me the heart to feel."[11]

2

More Basic Books

IN THIS CHAPTER are listed several sets of books that I wish every young minister would attempt to acquire according to the means at his disposal for purchasing books. Let me give them to you in chronological order.

First of all would be the three great sets of the church Fathers still available from Eerdmans: *The Ante-Nicene Fathers* in ten volumes; *The Nicene Fathers* in fourteen volumes, including the writings of Augustine and Chrysostom; and *The Post-Nicene Fathers* also in fourteen volumes, beginning with the epochal work of Eusebius. These great writings ought not only to be available in one's library, but they should be systematically read. For the next 1,200 years, there is nothing a Protestant minister must have until we come to the great commentaries of John Calvin, published first by the Calvin Translation Society in 1843-55 and now reprinted by Eerdmans in forty-five volumes.

Coming down to the middle of the nineteenth century, every serious student of the Scriptures should have a complete set of twenty-five volumes of the *Biblical Commentary on the Old Testament* by C. F. Keil and Franz Delitzsch. There is nothing to compare with Keil and Delitzsch.

As an indication of the profundity of the writings of Delitzsch, let me quote in part what he has to say about

a passage from which I am sure none of you have preached
and probably never will preach, the location of which I
suppose not one clergyman in a thousand could be sure
of without consulting the prophetic writings or a con-
cordance. Let me quote the words from the *New American Standard Bible*:

> So it will happen in that day, that the Lord will punish
> the host of heaven, on high, and the kings of the earth,
> on earth. And they will be gathered together *like* prison-
> ers in the dungeon, and will be confined in prison; and
> after many days they will be punished. Then the moon
> will be abashed and the sun ashamed, for the LORD of
> hosts will reign on Mount Zion and in Jerusalem, and
> *His* glory will be before His elders (Is 24:21-23).

Here is what Delitzsch has to say in part about this
passage:

> Hence the commentators are now pretty well agreed,
> that "the host on high" signifies here the angelic army.
> But it is self-evident, that a visitation of the angelic army
> cannot be merely a relative and partial one. And it is not
> sufficient to understand the passage as meaning the
> wicked angels, to the exclusion of the good. Both the
> context and the parallelism show that the reference must
> be to a penal visitation in the spiritual world, which
> stands in the closest connection with the history of man,
> and in fact with the history of the nations. Consequently
> the host on high will refer to the angels of the nations and
> kingdoms; and the prophecy here presupposes what is
> affirmed in Deuteronomy 32:8 (LXX.), and sustained in
> the book of Daniel, when it speaks of a *sar* of Persia,
> Javan, and even the people of Israel. . . . The reference
> is to the abyss of Hades, where they are reserved in chains
> of darkness unto the judgment of the great day. Accord-
> ing to this parallel, *yippakedu* (shall be visited) ought

apparently to be understood as denoting a visitation in wrath (like ch. 29:6, Ezekiel 38:8). . . . What the apocalyptist of the New Testament describes in detail in Revelation 20:4, 20:11 sqq., and 21., the apocalyptist of the Old Testament sees here condensed into one fact, viz. the enthroning of Jehovah and His people in a new Jerusalem, at which the silvery white moon (*lebanah*) turns red, and the glowing sun (*chammah*) turns pale; the two great lights of heaven becoming (according to a Jewish expression) "like a lamp at noonday" in the presence of such glory. . . . Rev. 20:4 (cf. Matthew 19:28) is a more appropriate parallel to the passage before us than Revelation 4:4, we may assume with certainty, at least with regard to this passage, and without needing to come to any decision concerning Revelation 4:4, that the *zekenim* here are not angels, but human elders after God's own heart. These elders, being admitted into the immediate presence of God, and reigning together with Him, have nothing but glory in front of them, and they themselves reflect that glory.[1]

No writer of this century, or any other, known to me, has actually recognized the profound eschatalogical meaning of this passage. As an example, contrast what I have just read from Delitzsch with Calvin's interpretation.

This passage has tortured the minds of many commentators, and various interpretations have been offered by various writers. Some think that this relates to the sun and the stars, and others, that it relates to the devils, who will be punished along with the wicked. Others refer it to the Jews, on whom God had bestowed a remarkable privilege. But I cannot adopt any of those interpretations. The simple and genuine meaning, therefore, appears to me to be, that no power will be so high as to be exempted from those scourges of God; and though they raise themselves above the clouds, yet the hand of

God will reach them; as it is said in the Psalm, "Whither shall I go from thy Spirit? and whither shall I flee from thy face? If I ascend into heaven, thou art there; if I take the wings of the morning, and dwell in the uttermost parts of the sea, there also shall thy hand pursue me" Psalm 139:7-10.[2]

In the latter part of the nineteenth century a work was published which is seldom seen today and almost never referred to, but which has the great virtue of giving detailed scholarly exposition of every phrase in the Old and New Testaments by the leading biblical scholars of that time. This is the twelve-volume work edited by F. C. Cook, *The Holy Bible with an Explanatory and Critical Commentary,* generally known as the *Speaker's Bible* (1871-88). It was in this series that Westcott's great commentary on the gospel of John first appeared.

At the beginning of the century appeared the truly great five-volume work, *The Expositor's Greek Testament* (1899-1910), edited by W. Roberston Nicoll, still available, published by Eerdmans. I cannot help but include here the greatest series of commentaries on the New Testament written in our century by an American scholar. This is *The Interpretation of the New Testament* by R. C. H. Lenski in 12 volumes, a Lutheran work, which will not fail to give illuminating help on every sentence of our glorious New Testament. Let me add at the end of this list a work which I hope most of you will gradually acquire, that is, the wonderful set of forty-five volumes of the sermons of Charles H. Spurgeon (1855-1905); and, if possible, one should secure, even if it is a xeroxed copy, the *index* to these sermons, which includes about 2,800 texts. These sermons easily represent the greatest evangelical preaching of the nineteenth century.

Finally, let me mention without any apology whatsoever, the greatest series of volumes of any one preacher of the nineteenth century except Spurgeon, the *Expositions of Holy Scripture* by Alexander Maclaren which was published in 1910. Nicoll says that "Maclaren had no time for the trivialities of life. He would not weary himself with speaking to total strangers after preaching. Committees depressed him, and he attended few of them. He was personally exceedingly shy and for this reason never was given to extensive pastoral visitation."[3]

In the fascinating volume, *Princes of the Church*, Nicoll paid the following great tribute to Maclaren. Nicoll knew more about this type of literature than any man of his generation.

> To him preaching was the exposition of the eternal divine thought. Anything else was not preaching. So the Bible was his book. Through his long life he was continually studying it in Hebrew and in Greek. Like Dale, in his latter days he put Westcott's commentaries above all the rest. Nothing interested him more in recent years than Dr. Moulton's New Testament Grammar, and the translation of the New Testament as affected by the discovery of the Greek papyri. All the wisdom of the world was to him contained in the Bible, but his business was to apply the Bible to life, and he read very widely in general literature. . . . Books of travel attracted him. He was a close student of history, and not ignorant of science. He studied the living book of humanity. His whole effort was to bring Bible truth into effective contact with the human heart. . . . He was a minister of the Word, a minister among the Baptists, faithful to the death, working in the inspiration of the early days to which his heart held firm. In this way he refused almost everything. He was always saying no. Every visitor whom he suspected of a new proposal was received at first with a certain gruff-

ness and suspicion, soon disarmed into smiling gentleness. His first book of sermons was simply dragged out of him. . . . It is difficult to believe that his Expositions of the Bible will be superseded. Will there ever again be such a combination of spiritual insight, of scholarship, of passion, of style, of keen intellectual power? He was clearly a man of genius, and men of genius are very rare. So long as preachers care to teach from the Scriptures they will find their best help and guide in him. That remains, but we who knew him know what has been taken from us as we recall the man, his heart, his voice, his mien, his accent, his accost. We shall not see his like again. We know also that in him as much power was kept back as was brought out. He did his work not merely for the time, but for the time to come. He spoke to those pierced with an anguish, "whose balsam never grew." He spoke to the cravings, to the aspirations, to the hopes as well as to the sorrows and the pains of humanity. The generations to come will care little or nothing for our sermons to the times, but they will listen to the sweet, clear voice of the man who preached to the end of Gilead—and Beulah—and the Gates of Day.[4]

SOME VERY IMPORTANT VOLUMES NOT COMMONLY KNOWN

After these many, many years of gathering a library, extensive reading, and the publishing of some bibliographies, I would like to call the attention of you young men to perhaps a dozen books that will be helpful in your interpreting the Holy Scriptures, but which are seldom seen today, some of them not even in many of our larger theological libraries, and strangely missing from contemporary bibliographies. Though they may be very difficult to purchase, these are not what we would call rare books and will not require an outlay of large sums. First of all, one of the most precious volumes on the deeper aspects of the teaching of Genesis is *Hebrew Ideals*, by James Strahan, at that time professor of Hebrew and Biblical Criticism in Magee College, Londonderry. His book called for four editions within twenty years. Let me just indicate the titles of some of these chapters: "Laughter" (21), "Love" (24), "Memory" (30-31), "Virtue" (39), "Farewell" (48-49).

Alexander Whyte preached the sermon at the induction of Strahan in the Belgrave Square Presbyterian Church, London, in which he said, "I expect every vacant seat will be filled to hear this reading, thinking, God-fearing young man. Have you read your minister's handbook for private studies, *Hebrew Ideals?* I have read it in proof, and again and again since it was printed. Let that fine piece of evangelical scholarship be in every house and make a gift of it to your reading men. Invite this reading man, young and old, to share your Sabbath here."[5]

I suppose that not many ministers today are undertaking a series of messages on the wonderfully rich types of Christ in the offerings set forth in the book of Leviticus, but when one does take courage to at least understand these offerings, the supreme book for that study, almost never referred to in bibliographies, is the large volume by Walter Stephen Moule, *The Offerings Made Like unto the Son of God* published in London in 1915, a work of great substance.

I am afraid we talk too easily about all of the Bible being inspired, and all of the Bible being profitable for meditation and for exposition. Yet how many areas, in spite of our own convictions, do we really neglect, even in a long ministry!! One of the larger books of the Old Testament, which a minister almost totally neglects, except for the story of Gideon, is the book of Judges. If a preacher should attempt a series of messages from these twenty-one chapters, some of them records of darkest deeds, he will find a preeminently rich work in *A Critical and Expository Commentary on the Book of Judges*, by A. R. Fausset, 1885, none other than the coauthor of that great commentary on the Bible by Jamieson, Fausset, and Brown. Fausset not only interprets the passages, but he draws rich spiritual teachings out of every paragraph, and then unfolds the practical application of every chapter as he concludes his exposition. It is a marvel of exposition.

In contrast to the general avoidance of the book of Judges, there are many volumes, generally small works, and some of them quite helpful, on the book of Ruth. Of these by far the richest is the significantly entitled volume, *Ruth the Satisfied Stranger*, by Philip Mauro. The one chapter on the meaning of *hap*, the root of our word *happened*, interpreting Ruth 2:3. "Her hap was to light on a part of the field," presents truths that most of us in reading the book of Ruth would never have even imagined.

Let me pass by the truly great commentaries on Psalms and the prophetic writings and mention but one volume on the book of Zechariah. I believe that the profoundest and richest and most refreshing exposition of any one of the minor prophets in our language is the one published at the beginning of our century, and often revised and reprinted, *The Visions and Prophecies by Zechariah*, by David Baron, a work of over 550 pages with indexes of subjects and Scripture passages of twenty-four and seventeen columns respectively. The volume should be in every Bible student's library.

While there are many books, some of them quite important, on the friends and companions of St. Paul, there is only one (known to me) that gives a complete list of all of these, with interesting scholarly notes on each of them. This list of ninety-nine men and women is found in *St.*

Paul and His Companions by E. Basil Redlich, published in London by Macmillan in 1913. One of the most interesting sections of this list is the three-page discussion of "the brother, whose praise is in the gospel" (2 Co 8:18). Not only is all the relevant New Testament material brought together here, but there are abundant references to postbiblical traditions, concerning many of these friends of St. Paul, some quite obscure.

All of us have found it more or less difficult to teach the epistle of James or to preach from its exhortations without seeming to be more or less superficial. Let me mention here a book rarely seen and totally ignored in bibliographies, yet easily the greatest exposition of this epistle in our language: *The Epistle of St. James* by H. Maynard Smith (Oxford, 1914).

CANDLISH ON 1 JOHN 5:19

My own opinion is that the richest exposition of the first epistle of John is still that series of lectures which Robert S. Candlish published in 1866, *The First Epistle of John Expounded in a Series of Lectures*. Candlish was for years the principal of the New College, and Minister of Free St. George's Church, Edinburgh. This volume became very scarce in the early part of our century, but fortunately it has since then been reprinted. As an illustration of the depths to which Candlish takes us in his exposition, may I quote three paragraphs from his chapter "The World Lieth in the Wicked One" (1 Jn 5:19).

> Considered in its origin, this lying of the world in the wicked one may be taken in a very literal and personal sense. The fall was a fall out of the arms of God into the embrace of the wicked one. He was ready to receive the fallen; and, in a measure, to break the fall. He has a bed of his own prepared on which the fallen may lie

in him. It is shrewdly and plausibly framed. It is like
himself. It is the embodiment of his mind and spirit;
the acting out of his very self. It is a couch composed of
the very materials he had before woven into the subtle
cord of that temptation which drew the fallen out of
God's hold into his. The same elements of unbelief which
he turned to such cunning account in his work of seduc-
tion, he employs with equal skill in getting the seduced to
lie, and to lie quiet, in him. For the most part, he finds this
an easy task. The world listens willingly to its seducer as
its comforter and guide; and frames its creed and con-
stitution according to his teaching, and under his inspiration. He is its doctor of divinity; its faith, worship, disci-
pline, and government are his. So the world lies in him,
dependent on him and his theology for such peace as it
has.

For the essence of worldliness is at bottom the feeling
that God's commandments are grievous; that his service
is hard, and himself austere; but yet that somehow his
indulgence may be largely reckoned upon in the end. It
is as lying in the wicked one that the world so conceives
of God, and acts upon that conception of him. It is as
lying in the wicked one that it peevishly asks, "Who
is the Almighty that we should serve him, and what
profit shall we have if we bow down unto him?"—while
at the same time it confidently presumes, "The Lord seeth
not, the Lord regardeth not."

The whole world thus lieth in the wicked one; he has
it all in his embrace; there is nothing in or about the world
that is not thus lying in the wicked one; so lying in him
as to be infected with the contagion of his hard thoughts
of God, and his affected bravery in defying judgment.

Take the world at its very best; all its grossness put
away; no vile lust or passion polluting it, much pure virtue adorning it; many pious sentiments coming forth from
it, not altogether insincerely. What trace is there here

of the wicked one's poisonous touch? What necessity for your being warned to be on your guard?

Nay, but look deeper into the heart of what is so seeming fair. Do you not see,—do you not instinctively feel,—that there is at bottom lacking in it that entire surrender of self to God; that unreserved owning of his sovereignty, the sovereignty of his throne, his law, his grace; that full, loyal, loving trust, which alone can baffle Satan's wiles? Instead of that, is there not a hidden fear of coming to too close quarters, and too confidential dealings with God; a disposition to stand aloof and make terms of compromise; a willingness to be persuaded that some questionable things may be tolerated, and some slight liberties allowed? Is not all this what "lying in the wicked one" may best explain?[6]

Of the hundreds, and I mean hundreds, of commentaries on the book of Revelation, let me not here attempt to tell you what is good and what is of no value at all. Instead may I commend a volume, published almost a hundred years ago, the equal of which has not been attempted in our language, *The Doctrine of the Apocalypse*, by Hermann Gebhardt, published in Edinburgh in an English translation in 1878. The book is exactly what the title indicates, a learned discussion of what the book of Revelation has to say about the Trinity, Christ, the church, the end of the age, angels, antichrist, Satan, hell, heaven, and judgment.

STANTON ON THE JEWISH AND CHRISTIAN MESSIAH

A volume which is quite difficult to come upon, but which an earnest student of the Scriptures should keep searching for, bears the significant title, *The Jewish and Christian Messiah*, by V. H. Stanton, Divinity Lecturer of Trinity College in Cambridge (Edinburgh, 1886). As rich

as the 400 pages of this book may be, what I especially
want to call to your attention is the marvelous folding chart
at the end of the book, "A Table Showing the Messianic
Use of the Old Testament in the New Testament." Stanton
places these references under six major headings and
over sixty minor headings! The Old Testament references
are in one column and the New Testament references in
the second column. If my estimates are correct, here you
have *classified and parallelled* 410 Old Testament references and 450 New Testament references of Messianic
significance. I know nothing else like this in the English
language.

HEATHEN CONTACT WITH CHRISTIANITY

All theological professors and many ministers are asked
if there were any references in secular literature to Christ
and the Christian faith within the one hundred years during and following the apostolic period? There is one small
volume of 120 pages that, as far as I know, is the only one
that records all such references, in Greek and Latin literature, down to 150 A.D. It is significantly entitled, *Heathen
Contact with Christianity During Its First Century and a
Half,* with the informing subtitle, *Being All References to
Christianity Recorded in Pagan Writings During that Period.* The author was C. R. Haines. Here you have both
the original Latin and Greek texts, with excellent translations and adequate footnotes.

Here I would like to insert the title of a book that does
not belong in this particular series of commentaries but is
something every minister will find of the greatest value.
The Children for Christ, by Andrew Murray, first published, I believe, in 1905, contains fifty-two rich, informing
studies, all based upon passages in the Old and New Testaments that have to do with children. What pastor does not

need to speak often to his people on some aspect of this important theme?

LEWIS ON RATIONALISM

It is strange how books can just disappear even within a quarter of a century in which they are originally published. In 1913 S.P.C.K. published a work of the greatest value which became so scarce that I have never even seen it listed in a secondhand book catalog during the last thirty years, and most theological seminary libraries do not possess it. In fact, I do not recall seeing this listed in any bibliography of Christian apologetics even though it stands by itself among biographical studies of unbelievers. The title of this book, by Henry Lewis, indicates exactly what the volume contains: *Modern Rationalism as Seen at Work in Its Biographies.* This is a carefully documented study with an apparatus of footnotes indicating a thorough first-hand acquaintance with the relevant literature of the tragic consequences attending rationalistic convictions in the lives of Voltaire, Thomas Paine, John Stuart Mill, Renan, Bradlaugh, Herbert Spencer, and Nietzsche, with briefer discussions of Goethe, Schopenhauer, Shelley, et cetera, and a chapter on "Agnosticism and the Experience Which Death Brings."

I wish someone would do a work for this late twentieth century such as Lewis did for some of these noted rationalists of the nineteenth century.

WALKER ON ACTS

Some years ago my beloved friend, the late Fred Mitchell, then home director of the China Inland Mission, asked me if I had a copy of *The Acts of the Apostles* by the famous missionary to India, Thomas Walker. I told him I had never even heard of the book but would try to get a copy.

I began at once to inquire around for one, all to no avail. Each time Mitchell saw me, he asked if I had yet secured a copy of Walker, to which I was compelled to reply in the negative.

The book was published in 1910 and reprinted in 1919, appearing in the Indian Church Commentary series published by S.P.C.K. I finally persuaded Moody Press to publish a reprint of this work, for which I wrote a biographical preface; however, the book has been withdrawn from the publisher's list. Personally I consider this the greatest commentary on the book of Acts written from a missionary standpoint that has been published in our language. The author was a careful student of the Greek text. The introduction includes a rich section on "Lessons of the Acts for the Indian Church," which can well be applied to missionary work in other countries. Each chapter concludes with a most helpful summary of the teachings of that particular portion of the Word of God. I have never seen this book listed in any bibliography, but it is a treasure house indeed, with much material not to be found in any other commentary on Acts. I urge young men to keep searching until a copy is in their own library.

A TOPICAL ANALYSIS OF PROPHECY

I think this is the place to mention that remarkable topical analysis of the subject of prophecy, which appears in the *Syntopicon,* the index to the *Great Books of the Western World.* Here the subject of prophecy is divided as follows: (1) the nature and power of prophecy; (2) the vocation of prophecy: the possession of foreknowledge; (3) the varieties of prophecy and the instruments of divination; (4) particular prophecies of hope and doom; (5) the criticism and rejection of prophecy: the distinction between true and false prophecy.

The first division is divided into four sections with abundant references to ten authors of the ancient world from Homer to Plutarch and then references to Shakespeare, Gibbon, Hegel, Goethe, Freud, et cetera.

3

The Greatest Theme of All –
The Person and Work
of the Lord Jesus Christ

THE MOST INEXHAUSTIBLE, inspiring, and important subject that can ever occupy the minds of men is the person and work of Jesus Christ. Even the aspects of His person make Him unique among the great men of history—preexistence, incarnation, deity, resurrection, ascension, and the second advent—as do the glorious titles that are ascribed to Him—Son of God, the Lamb of God, the Way, the Truth, the Life, and the Saviour.

Let me share the opening paragraph of Andrew Fairbairn's *Studies in the Life of Christ*:

> The greatest problems in the field of history centre in the Person and Life of Christ. Who He was, and what He was, how and why He came to be it, are questions that have not lost and will not lose their interest for us and for mankind. For the problems that centre in Jesus have this peculiarity: they are not individual, but general—concern not a person, but the world. How we are to judge Him is not simply a curious point for historical criticism, but a vital matter for religion. Jesus Christ is the most powerful spiritual force that ever operated for good on and in humanity. He is today what He has been for centuries—an object of reverence and love to the good, the cause of remorse and change, penitence and hope to the bad; of moral strength to the morally weak,

of inspiration to the despondent, consolation to the desolate, and cheer to the dying. He has created the typical virtues and moral ambitions of civilized man; has been to the benevolent a motive to beneficence, to the selfish a persuasion to self-forgetful obedience; and has become the living ideal that has steadied and raised, awed and guided youth, braced and ennobled manhood, mellowed and beautified age. In Him the Christian ages have seen the manifested Good, the Eternal living in time, the Infinite within the limits of humanity; and their faith has glorified His sufferings into a sacrifice by the Creator for the creature, His death into an atonement for human sin. No other life has done such work, no other person been made to bear such transcendent and mysterious meanings. It is impossible to touch Jesus without touching millions of hearts now living and yet to live. He is whatever else He may be, as a world's imperishable wonder, a world's everlasting problem, as a pre-eminent object of human faith, a pre-eminent subject of human thought.[1]

How many volumes have been written directly relating to the Lord Jesus Christ, probably no one knows. In 1906 Samuel Gardiner Ayres published his well-known *Jesus Christ Our Lord, an English Bibliography of Christology,* in which he listed more than five thousand different books concerning the Lord Jesus Christ, available in English prior to the beginning of the twentieth century. I suppose one could safely say that over ten thousand books have been written about the Lord Jesus Christ in English during the last two hundred years. The number written in German, French, Italian, and other European languages has never been tabulated, as far as I know. Thus it is very important, for a student who has the means to purchase only a few books of Christ and for all students whose limited time enables them to master only a few great books in this important field, to purchase and study only those works which are of permanent significance, and can be looked upon as authoritative.

Probably the one life of Christ which has been more extensively used than any other in our language is the famous *The Life and Times of Jesus the Messiah* by Dr. Alfred Edersheim.* Born of Jewish parentage, Edersheim was living in England when he was converted to Christianity under the influence of the Scotch Presbyterian chaplain, John Duncan. Returning with him to Scotland, Edersheim studied theology at New College, Edinburgh, and at the University of Berlin. At the age of 21 he was ordained as a Presbyterian minister. In 1875 he became a clergyman of the Church of England, and he lectured at Oxford University from 1884 to 1890. In some ways this book will probably never be surpassed, especially in showing the reader how Jewish customs of Christ's day and contemporary Hebrew literature illuminate many of the teachings which were uttered by the Saviour. Even such a severe critic as Driver said of this book that it was "a monument of learning, presented in an immediate readable form, and a storehouse of information on every subject which comes within its range."[2] Let no minister think he is being economical by purchasing the abridged one-volume edition. If one has to wait a year, wait and get the two-volume edition, which is the only one which has all the virtues of this great work.

In 1862 Samuel J. Andrews published the first edition of his *The Life of Our Lord Upon the Earth Considered in Its Historical, Chronological and Geographical Relations.* Edition after edition was called for. In 1891 a new and wholly revised edition was issued, which stands even today as one of the most important single volumes on the life of Christ

---

*First published in 1883. As far as I know, the last edition was the 8th, 1903, with a total of over 1,500 pages.

ever written.† Marcus Dods, a famous author who was as well acquainted with the New Testament literature in Germany and Britain as probably any man of his day said of Andrews' volume, "This work is indispensable to any one who intends a thorough study of the subject, but yet has not access to the authorities themselves, or has not leisure to use them. The accuracy of his references, and impartiality of his citations, as well as the fairness and candor of his own judgments, inspire us with confidence in the author."[3]

In some ways the most monumental life of Christ that has been written in any language is the one by the famous commentator, John Peter Lange, published in English under the title, *The Life and Times of the Lord Jesus Christ* (4 vols., Edinburgh, 1872).‡ The last two volumes were edited by Dods. These volumes are by one of the outstanding conservative theologians and New Testament scholars of the last half century in Germany. The work is profound, theological, reverent, tremendously suggestive, occasionally perhaps a little tedious, but never failing to move and inspire the careful reader—indeed, so much so, that one cannot read more than twenty or thirty pages of the work at a time. I have found, in referring to this work during the years, that comparatively few people in our country have come to know it, which leads me to lay added stress upon its greatness. I do not know anything to compare with it in this particular field.

Probably the most widely read biography of Christ originating in English early in our century is *The Days of His Flesh* by David Smith. Strange to say no important life of Christ was written by an American scholar throughout the

---

†I had the privilege of writing a biographical introduction for the Zondervan reprint of 1954.

‡The entire work extends to something over 2,000 pages. Dods wrote a very illuminating preface for this translation.

century from Andrews until Everett Harrison published his *Short Life of Christ* in 1968. Harrison reveals himself abreast of the latest literature as indicated by the fact that he quotes books by New Testament scholars published as late as 1966. The review in the *Westminster Theological Journal* concludes by saying that this volume "deserves not only to be an evangelical classic, . . . but indeed a classic as a life of Christ that will profit every reader."[4] Its thoroughness may be seen in that over 1,000 verses are listed in its index to scripture passages.

The work that was most widely used of all writings of this kind was G. Campbell Morgan's *The Crises of the Christ* (1903), in which he discussed unforgettably the seven great epochs of our Lord's life: His birth, baptism, temptation, transfiguration, crucifixion, resurrection, and ascension. This did not exercise so much influence among New Testament scholars, as for example, the writings of William Sanday, but it did have, and continues to have, an enormous influence over ministers and those who are teaching the gospels. It is Morgan's greatest book, published when he was only forty years of age. Seventy years later it is still used as a textbook in many schools and even seminaries.

It is significant that Roman Catholic scholars have in the last fifty years produced many more important biographies of Jesus than the Protestants, most of them first being published in French as those by M. J. Lagrange (1930); J. Lebreton (1931); L. de Grandmaison (18th ed. 1931); and Ferdinand Pratt (1950 from the 16th French edition). The largest of all these works is by L. C. Fillion, *The Life of Christ*, first appearing in 1945, costing the learned author six years of labor, a work of over 2,100 pages including sixty-nine appendixes and an index of Scripture references numbering over 5,400. We think of France as more or less of a nation of skeptics and agnostics, but we must admit that no life of Christ written by any British or American scholar in the last one hundred years has reached as many as 15 or 18 editions, which some of these French biographies have attained.§

Before proceeding further in this literature about Christ, may I call attention to a strange phenomenon among ministers—the mysterious neglect of studying the life of Jesus Christ. A few years ago I happened to be speaking in one of the most important evangelical churches of North America, of which the gifted pastor is now about fifty years of age. The opportunity of looking over his library led me to make the remark, "I do not see any volume on the life and work of Jesus in your library."

This seemed to take him by surprise, and then he acknowledged, "Well, I guess I don't have any book on the life of Christ." Preaching the gospel for a quarter of a century to large congregations, a man well-informed on prophecy and earnest in the matter of missions, has no life of Christ in his own library! I am referring to this not because it is something rare, but rather, I am afraid the same can be said of a great many ministers of our generation.

One of the most remarkable books on the Lord Jesus published during the twentieth century is not too well known to this generation of clergy and Christians as a whole. It is significantly entitled *The Walk, Conversation, and Character of Jesus Christ Our Lord,* a series of thirty-five Sabbath evening addresses by that greatly gifted preacher of Edinburgh, Alexander Whyte. I cannot speak of this book too highly. It is one of those rare volumes that I would urge every minister in the English world to pos-

§Among the other Roman Catholic authors of lives of Christ, all of them in two volumes, were the Abbé Constant Fouard (London, 1891); Father Didon, 3rd ed. (London, 1895); Alban Goddier (New York, 1944); and Maurice Meschler (St. Louis, 1953).

sess. He will be reading scores of books about Christ and the gospels that do not begin to communicate the inspiration that radiates from these pages. I would like to quote whole chapters of this rich volume, but will confine myself to his words based on Luke 3:21-22. "Now it came to pass, when all the people were baptized, that, Jesus also having been baptized, and praying, the heaven was opened, and the Holy Spirit descended in a bodily form, as a dove, upon him, and a voice came out of heaven, Thou art my beloved Son; in thee I am well pleased" (ASV).

It is to the third Evangelist that we are indebted for this fine information that it was when Jesus was praying that the heaven was opened. Our Lord prayed without ceasing, but there were times and places when He prayed more earnestly, and His baptism was one of those times and places. What all His thoughts were as He descended under the water and came up again out of it is far too deep for us to wade out into; at the best we can but adoringly guess at His thoughts and at His prayer. May His prayer at that moment not have been that He might receive the Holy Ghost without measure so as to seal Him with all possible certitude to His great office, and so as to guide Him with all possible clearness as to how and when He was to enter on it? We can safely guess at His unrecorded prayer from the answer He immediately received to His prayer. For while He was yet speaking, the heaven opened and the answer to His prayer came down. My brethren, will nothing teach you to pray? Will all His examples, and all His promises, and all your own needs, and cares, and distresses, not teach you to pray? What hopeless depravity must there be in your heart when, with all He can do, God simply cannot get you to come to Him in prayer.[5]

A voice came from heaven which said, Thou art My beloved Son; in whom I am well pleased. Think of it, my brethren. Never once since the fall of Adam and Eve had the Maker of men been able to say these words till He said them to Jesus Christ that day at the Jordan. Almighty God had often looked down from heaven to see if there were any that did good and sinned not. But when His eyelids tried the children of men it was always with the same result. Not one. Not Noah, not Abraham, not Jacob, not Joseph, not Moses, not David; no not one single patriarch or prophet, or psalmist, or saint, in all the house of Israel. But here at least is a man after God's own heart. Here at last is the second Adam, with whom God is well pleased. Listen well to these words,—"Well pleased." Think with all your might Who pronounces these words, and over Whom they are pronounced. Think, also, what all these words mean in His mouth who utters them, and in His ears, and in His heart, who hears them. And then, having thought all that well over; be entirely selfish for once. Turn to yourself and think what blessed words these words, "well pleased," are for you. Think it out how these words bear on you, and how these words come all the way from the Jordan to belong to you. Think continually of what these words absolutely secure and seal down for ever to you. As, also, what they expect and claim of you. For one thing, these words, "I am well pleased with My beloved Son," expect and demand of you that you shall as never before be very ill-pleased with yourself. . . . But if there is nothing and no one on the face of the whole earth who ever causes you so much pain and disappointment and dissatisfaction and displeasure as you continually cause yourself, then you are the very man to go straight to the Jordan, and to accompany Christ through all that baptism scene of His for you. Do not despair of yourself though you are far worse pleased with yourself tonight than ever you were before. Do not despair of yourself so long as the Jordan runs in your New Testament. . . . If you can look on

Jesus the Christ coming up out of the water praying for Himself and for you as your Mediator, and if you will take home to your heart of hearts these glorious words spoken over Him by His Father, then His Father is well pleased with you henceforth, for His righteousness sake. And what more would you have? What more, what better, could God Himself do for you, or for any man, than to proclaim you accepted in His beloved Son. Beyond that even God cannot go. Beseech Him then to go that length with you and with me tonight.[6]

Of all the anthologies of Jesus—and there are many of them—the one that embraces the greatest rarities of literature is the *Anthology of Jesus* edited by Sir James Marchant (Harpers, 1926), containing 422 different items with full references for each of them. It is in this volume that one will find the exact account of a story that has been variously repeated from generation to generation.

A COMPANY of English literary men, including Charles Lamb, Hazlitt, Leigh Hunt, and others one day fell to discussing persons they would like to have met, and after naming every possible name in the gallery of fame, whether worthy or unworthy, Charles Lamb said in his stuttering way to the company: "There is only one person I can ever think of after this. . . . If Shakespeare was to come into this room, we should all rise up to meet him; but if that person was to come into it we should all fall and try to kiss the hem of His garment."[7]

It is probably here we should mention a harmony of the gospels. Of all those that have been published, I think that the one that is still most convenient and helpful is *A Harmony of the Gospels for Historical Study* edited by William A. Stevens and Ernest DeWitt Burton. It first appeared in 1893, and required eleven editions within a score of years. There is a most interesting remark in this volume which one would hardly expect to come out of the University of Chicago in the early part of our century. The editors tell us in the preface:

> It is not to be forgotten that thus far every effort to accentuate their disagreement has only strengthened the impression of their concord as historical documents. The most powerful of all arguments for the substantial truthfulness of the witnessing evangelists is to be found in the self-consistency and verisimilitude of the history, when exhibited in a harmony constructed according to the principles indicated in this preface. If, after a century of modern criticism of the gospels, it is found that, despite all differences, the four mutually supplement and mutually interpret one another, so that from their complex combination there emerges *one* narrative, outlining a distinct historical figure, and producing upon the mind an irresistible impression of reality, it is difficult to imagine a more convincing attestation of the records on which the Christian church bases its faith in the person and work of its Founder than is furnished by this very fact.‖, 8

Rather than attempt brief notices of books on the major aspects of our Lord's incarnate life, let me rather devote these paragraphs to books relating exclusively to the *death* of our Lord. First of all, each minister's library should have at least one volume on the cross as an instrument of crucifixion. The preeminent work is *The Cross in Tradition, History, and Art* by William W. Seymour, a superb volume of quarto size of over 500 pages with 270 illustrations and a remarkable bibliography of 300 titles. For a brief but profound consideration of the various events of that epochal day, there is nothing better than *The Trial and Death of Jesus Christ* by James Stalker (1894).

‖There should also be mentioned here *A Harmony of the Synoptic Gospels in Greek* by E. D. Burton and E. J. Goodspeed.

For meditations on each event and each utterance of this forever hallowed day, the outstanding work is *The Suffering Saviour* by the greatest preacher in Europe in the middle of the nineteenth century, F. W. Krummacher, reaching the eighth edition in English by 1856. This book became very scarce, and I had the privilege of editing a reprint and writing a biographical preface for it (Chicago: Moody, 1953). I am told that when this volume came into the possession of some ministers they soon were reading it on their knees.

A volume rarely seen today, but of abiding value, is *The Cross of Christ* by Otto Zoeckler (London, 1877) a work of great learning, with chapters on such subjects as Constantine's vision of the cross, the cross in the church of the Middle Ages, the cross in the theology and church of the reformation, and the sign of the returning son of man. A volume that every minister ought to have in his library, sermonically rich and not too scarce, is *The Day of the Cross* by W. M. Clow.

One cannot discuss the cross of Christ without being led immediately to the great theme of atonement. Of the scores of really important books, I will mention only the following.

The work that exercised a tremendous influence in the Christian church at the beginning of this century was *The Death of Christ: Its Place and Interpretation in the New Testament* (London, 1902) by James Denney.

Then there are two volumes by George Smeaton that should be on the shelves of every believing student of the New Testament. They were published nearly one hundred years ago, but within the last twenty years have been reprinted. I am referring to *The Doctrine of the Atonement as Taught by Christ Himself*, and *The Doctrine of the Atonement as Taught by the Apostles*. Here are mature theological discussions of every verse in the New Testament that relates to the sacrificial death of our Lord. More recently the liberal theologian Vincent Taylor has had four different volumes published (1945-1956). *The Christian Doctrine of Atonement in New Testament Teaching; The Cross of Christ; Forgiveness and Reconciliation;* and *Jesus and His Sacrifice.* A book that has had most favorable acceptance by a contemporary scholar is *The Apostolic Preaching of the Cross* by Leon Morris (1955). A volume that is today rarely seen, and not referred to in most modern bibliographies, is *The Philosophy of the Cross,* by Robert M'Cheyne Edgar. This volume, full of rich things, deserves careful study.

I began by insisting that I would not introduce books on the other great subjects related to our Lord's life apart from His death, but there are two volumes I just must mention in passing. Both of them have been out of print for some time. One is by B. B. Warfield, *The Lord of Glory.* With characteristic thoroughness he discusses the great titles given Jesus by Himself and by the early church.

I have frequently developed bibliographies on the resurrection, but must pass these by except to mention one volume that has become quite scarce and is seen in only an occasional seminary library: *The Gospel of A Risen Saviour* by R. M'Cheyne Edgar (Edinburgh, 1892). This volume shows a full acquaintance with all the significant German, French, English, and American literature on the subject, and grapples with so many related subjects not found in most books on the resurrection that it is to be regretted that some publisher has not reprinted it. In some ways it is the most satisfying volume in English on the spiritual aspects of the resurrection. His chapters "The Demonstration of the Spirit—Christ Risen in the History of the Church"; "The Demonstration of the Critics—the Risen

Turner, H. E. W. *Jesus Master and Lord.* 1953. "A judicious, moderate, and mainly conservative estimate of recent studies on the Gospels, with bibliographies."

STUDIES IN CHRISTOLOGY

Berkouwer, G. C. *The Person of Christ.* 1954.
———. *The Work of Christ.* 1969.
Bochert, Otto. *The Original Jesus.* 1933.
Cave, Sydney. *The Doctrine of the Work of Christ.* 1937.
———. *Doctrine of the Person of Christ.*
Cawley, Frederick. *The Transcendence of Jesus Christ.* 1936. With a helpful bibliography.
Franks, Robert S. *A History of the Doctrine of the Work of Christ.* 1925. Two volumes of massive scholarship.
Gogarten, Friedrich. *Christ the Crises.* 1970. English translation.
Gore, Charles. *The Incarnation of the Son of God.* 1891.
———. *Belief in Christ.* 1922.
———. *Jesus of Nazareth.* 1929.
Henry, Carl F. H., ed. *Jesus of Nazareth: Saviour and Lord.* 1966. Chapters by outstanding scholars on sixteen subjects relating to Christ.
Morton, John Stewart. *Conflict in Christology.* 1947. With a bibliography of over 300 titles.
Ottley, R. L. *The Doctrine of the Incarnation.* 1908.
Relton, H. L. *A Study in Christology.* 1917.
Thomas, W. H. Griffith. *Christianity Is Christ.* 1946. Most suggestive.
Thornton, L. S. *The Incarnate Lord.* 1926.
Warfield, Benjamin Breckenridge. *The Lord of Glory.* 1907. On the names of Christ.

SURVEYS OF THE TREATMENT OF CHRIST IN THE NINETEENTH AND TWENTIETH CENTURIES

Kepler, Thomas S., comp. *Contemporary Thinking about Jesus: An Anthology.* 1944. Extracts from the brief biographies of fifty-four authors.

Latouche, E. Digges. *The Person of Christ in Modern Thought.* 1912.

McCown, C. C. *The Search for the Real Jesus: A Century of Historical Study.* 1940.

Woods, H. G. *Jesus in the Twentieth Century.* 1960.

There are a number of collections of sayings about Christ. In addition to the Marchant volume mentioned earlier in the chapter, one of the most comprehensive is the one edited by Ralph Louis Woods, *Behold the Man: An Anthology of Jesus Christ,* 1941.

Of an altogether different character is a volume published in Jerusalem, 1963, by the Franciscan Custody of the Holy Land, *The Life of Christ in the Sites and Monuments of Palestine,* with probably 600 illustrations.

4

The History and Influence of the Bible

THERE ARE SIX MAJOR AREAS of investigation, study, and research in relation to this precious Book, the Bible. Let me refer briefly to five of these, and then devote most of this chapter to the sixth area of study in relation to the Scriptures—the *influence* of the Bible.

There is first the matter of *inscription,* by which is meant the original writing by the authors of the various books of the Bible, under divine direction, and often, as Luke tells us, as the result of careful investigation. This includes the forever important matters of revelation and inspiration. While it is true that holy men of God spoke as they were moved by the Holy Spirit (2 Pe 1:21), of the actual process of writing, either the books of the Old Testament or the New, we have very little information. Of course, they could only write in the language which they knew. Most of the Old Testament was written in the Hebrew language, and the New Testament in the Greek language. The composition of the Old Testament literature stretches over a period of at least 800 years, from the Mosaic period to the last of the Old Testament prophets, Malachi, while the New Testament writings all may be assigned to the first century of our era.

The second great area of study is that of *canonization,* the assignment of certain books to a place of preeminence and recognition of their divine origin—a very complicated

68

matter. In fact, just how certain writings of the Old Testament period came to be acknowledged as truly of God, and how the New Testament church gradually recognized certain books as apostolic and inspired, and relegated other contemporary literature to a lower category, raises many problems. After Israel finally agreed upon what books were to be included in the law, the prophets, and the Psalms, and the early church decided what books belonged in the canon of inspired writings, there inevitably arose the problem of *preservation*. All of these writings, of course, were handwritten in manuscript form. Many of them were written on material that ultimately would disintegrate. It has been over 1,800 years since the *last* page of the divine writings was inscribed. Remembering that during the subsequent centuries both Israel and the church have often suffered vicissitudes of various kinds, such as persecution involving flight and the destruction of churches and monasteries, one is immediately aware of what we might well call the miracle of the preservation of these holy writings. Who possessed them? Who kept them? Who saw that they were copied from century to century?

With the worldwide scattering of the Hebrew people and the amazing extension of the Christian church in one city after another in the Roman Empire, with millions of people unable to read the original Hebrew and Greek, there came the necessity for *translation*. That subject itself has occupied the entire life of many devout scholars.

With authentic copies of the Scriptures in our hands, there arises the absolute need of *interpretation*—the ascertaining, first of all, of the meaning of the words of the Hebrew Bible and the Greek New Testament, and then for each translation the meaning of the words of the language that certain nations can understand. Out of this arises that vast literature of lexicons, Hebrew and Greek dictionaries, and then the thousands of volumes of commentaries, of systematic and dogmatic theologies, and of the social and economic life of those who are portrayed in these ancient books.

Here are five major subjects that need continued investigation, around some of which an entire library has been produced—inscripturation, canonization, preservation, translation, and interpretation.

Finally, there is the equally vast area for the study of the *influence* of the Scriptures in Israel, in the days of our Lord, in the early church, and in subsequent centuries. This includes the influence of the Bible in religion and creeds, in the areas of art, music, and liturgy, the enormous influence of the life of Christ as portrayed in the gospels, hope engendered in the hearts of men and women, the influence of the Bible in legislation and government, the relation of the Bible to missions, its use in preaching, and (a subject that can never be wholly exhausted) the power of the Word of God in the lives of individual men and women.

A number of more or less important studies have appeared during these last few decades concerning the influence and use of the Bible in English literature. Professor Busch of Harvard once said that a complete study of the influence of the Bible in English literature alone would be beyond the capacity of any one scholar in a lifetime of work. It is not my purpose here even to list some of these volumes, but I would call your attention to two items that may escape your attention. Before I do so, may I tease you by mentioning a book which I have not been able to acquire, after years of searching! If you should happen to have such good fortune as to possess the volume, may I remind you that it really belongs in *my* library, not in *yours!* The title of this book of over 300 pages is *The*

Bible in Waverly, or Sir Walter Scott's Use of Sacred Scripture, by N. Dickson (Edinburgh: Longmans, 1884).

The most complete *bibliography* of the Bible in English literature is known today only to specialists, and deserves a wider circulation. It is entitled *Biblical Influence in English Literature. A Survey of Studies* published in 1953 by the author, Henrietta Tichy, at the time on the faculty of Hunter College.

A series of volumes known as the *Temple Bible* has been published in pocket size, 4 by 5 inches. Each is edited by some outstanding biblical scholar and published in London by J. M. Dent in 1902. At the end of each of these volumes is a remarkable appendix, "Biblical References in English Literature." Thus, for example, the small volume on Genesis contains in the appendix 140 references to the use of various passages in the book of Genesis in English literature. James Moffatt issued seven small books at the beginning of our century with the general title, *Literary Illustrations of the Bible,* material which first appeared in the *Expositor* (6th ser., vol. 10 and 11).

No one and no group probably will ever be able to compose a series of volumes that will fully describe even all the basic data belonging to these subjects, even though hundreds of books have been written on one or the other of them. For ourselves, we have had to wait until the last twenty years for any major attempt at a work embracing all these themes. I am referring to the unique and brilliantly edited three-volume work, *The Cambridge History of the Bible.* The three volumes published from 1963-70 carry the following titles: *From the Beginning to Jerome, The West from the Fathers to the Reformation, The West from the Reformation to the Present Day.* It is with this three-volume work that I will occupy the rest of this chapter.

Even in the titles of the last two volumes, one recognizes that the work does not cover all the areas occupied by the Christian church. May I give some statistics here as an indication of the exhaustiveness of these volumes? The chapters are written by forty-seven authorities, a few from the Continent have written short chapters on various continental versions, three of them are American scholars (two from Yale and one from the University of Chicago), while the rest are British. The three volumes embrace 1,800 pages in which are included 1,540 titles in various bibliographies, with indexes listing 3,000 texts and 5,500 subjects, an encyclopedic work indeed as even such statistics indicate.

There are so many important statements in this book, and so many subjects touched upon, that one finds it difficult as to what to select. The first volume begins with four sections of a basic nature, namely, "The Biblical Languages," "The Biblical Scripts," "Books in the Ancient Near East and in the Old Testament" (by Donald J. Wiseman of the University of London), and "Books in the Graeco-Roman World and in the New Testament." Even here are some interesting statements. For instance, "In the *Iliad* writing is referred to only once, and in the *Odyssey* not even once, in the Bible we find as many as 429 references to writing or written documents."[1]

The age of writing in the ancient world has been pushed back into a period little dreamed of at the end of the nineteenth century. The volume we are considering reminds us that as early as 3100 B.C. "in Mesopotamia, and soon thereafter in Egypt, Anatolia and Elam, *scribes* were at work in the principal cities and centres of government." Our author then makes a statement which would be impossible fifty years ago that "By the time of Moses eight different languages were recorded in five different writing-systems. The development of a simple 22-letter system must soon have led to widespread literacy."[2]

There are some statements here that really deserve to be inscribed on the margin of one's Bible, for example, this superb testimony to the uniqueness of the Pauline epistles: "What has still to be explained is why no one previous to Paul had written letters of this kind, and why no one was to do so after him. We have no other examples of a man, even a Christian missionary, entangling himself with others in such a way as to produce an exchange of letters of this kind."[3]

The significance of the Qumran discoveries are frequently revealed in these pages. What they reveal about the position of Daniel in the first century before Christ will compel some rewriting on the authenticity of that book in the years to come. "Fragments of at least seven different manuscripts of Daniel have been discovered. . . . It seems, therefore, reasonable to conclude that the Qumran community not only used and highly valued the book of Daniel, but recognised it as having canonical authority. . . . The texts of Daniel which have been discovered appear not to have included the additions to the book which are found in the Greek text."[4]

The whole problem of eschatology in the first century will now have to be reconsidered. C. K. Barrett of Durham University reminds us:

> Their [those of the Qumran community] interpretation of the Old Testament was determined by their conviction that they lived in the appointed time in which the words of the prophets became historical fact. . . .
>
> As we turn, however, to the New Testament, no observation about the use of the Old Testament in the Qumran Scrolls is so important as that their authors believed that the prophets wrote not of their own time but of the time

of the End, and that they, the community, lived at the time of the End, that they themselves, and their deeds, were the fulfilment of scripture.[5]

May I here introduce an item from the second volume relating to this matter of one's believing he was at the end of the age. In writing about the study of the Bible in medieval Judaism, Dr. E. I. J. Rosenthal, of the University of Cambridge, refers to a book by Don Isaac Abravanel (1437-1509), a commentary on Daniel, which I think has never been translated. The statement of this learned Hebraist of conditions in the fifteenth century is as follows:

> That in the midst of all the anguish and persecutions many of our nation leave the religious community and this is heresy, for through the wickedness of the nations hundreds of thousands of Jews have forcibly left the Lord . . . *until all kingdoms are changed to heresy* shows that this refers to all nations in general or to the wicked in particular, be it to Rome where our own eyes see in the kingdom of Spain that heretics increase and where they burn them because of their heresy *in thousands and myriads.* . . . Also all the priests and bishops of Rome in this time run after profit, accept bribes and do not care for their religion.[6]

To this our author adds:

> These were clear signs that the Messiah would soon come and with him the end of the exile and the promised redemption. The prophecy of Daniel was about to be fulfilled. Rome, the fourth empire, was full of sin and corruption; it staggered to its destruction. Then the fifth empire, that of the king Messiah, would dawn upon mankind and bring redemption to the righteous of the Jews and of all nations.[7]

It would be interesting to make a careful study of what

Jewish commentators on Daniel thought about their own age, as being predicted by Daniel, and persuading them they were at the end of the world.

There is an interesting statement by St. Augustine which I never tire of repeating to any seminary class I might be teaching:

> Hasty and careless readers are led astray by many and manifold obscurities and ambiguities, substituting one meaning for another; and in some places they cannot hit upon even a fair interpretation. Some of the expressions are so obscure as to shroud the meaning in the thickest darkness. And I do not doubt that all this was divinely arranged for the purpose of subduing pride by toil and of preventing a feeling of satiety in the intellect, which generally holds in small esteem what is discovered without difficulty. . . .
>
> Whoever then thinks that he understands the holy scriptures or any part of them, but puts such an interpretation upon them as does not tend to build up this twofold love of God and of our neighbor, does not yet understand them as he ought.[8]

There is a significant remark in the early part of this volume that calls attention to a very simple fact which we are prone to forget. "Though the teacher himself need not be a writer of books any more than Jesus himself was, yet his activity implied that books were readily available. Christianity grew up with the idea, quite alien to the pagan world, that books were an essential part of religion."[9]

We should remember in discussing the text and canon of the Old Testament that

> Any account of the development of the text prior to c. 300 B.C., i.e. in the Persian period, not to mention the periods of the Babylonian Exile or of the First Temple, must perforce rely upon conjecture and, at best, upon deductions

and analogies derived from later literature and later manuscripts. . . . In fact not one single verse of this ancient
literature has come to us in an original manuscript, written by a biblical author or by a contemporary of his, or
even by a scribe who lived immediately after the time of
the author. Even the very earliest manuscripts at our disposal, in Hebrew or in any translation language, are removed by hundreds of years from the date of origin of
the literature recorded in them.[10]

While, of course, Origen had many heretical views, nevertheless, his influence was enormous, probably greater
than any other biblical scholar of those early centuries.
And, what will surprise many, it was Origen who continually insisted that the Scriptures were inspired by the Holy
Spirit.

> For Origen's belief in the Holy Spirit's inspiration of scrip-
> ture implied that it was true not simply in the broad, gen-
> eral drift of its teaching but in the most minute detail of
> its intended meaning. . . . Origen held to a view of ver-
> bal inspiration of a most rigorous kind. . . .
>
> If the Holy Spirit is the author of all scripture, it fol-
> lows that every detail is significant since God does nothing
> in vain. But it also follows that the meaning of every part
> must be in full agreement with the meaning of every other
> part, since God never contradicts himself. . . .
>
> The Holy Spirit is the true author of scripture; the
> Holy Spirit therefore is the indispensable source of a true
> understanding of its meaning. . . .
>
> His conviction of the inescapable necessity of the Holy
> Spirit's guidance for the work of scriptural interpreta-
> tion goes hand in hand with a readiness to pursue the
> most detailed textual or lexicographical research in the
> interests of a more precise exegesis. Just as in the inspira-
> tion of scripture the Holy Spirit does not bypass the hu-
> man mind but enhances its capacities, so with its inter-

pretation it is the divine Logos making his abode within the human mind who imparts to that mind the spiritual insight which it needs. . . .

Origen's beliefs about the Holy Spirit's guidance did not lead him to skimp the hard work required of the would-be interpreter of the spiritual message of the Bible. But just as his belief in the Holy Spirit's authorship of scripture gave him a false expectancy that there were always detailed spiritual meanings to be found at every point within it, so his belief in the Holy Spirit's aid in the task of interpreting gives him at times a false confidence that he is in the process of finding them. . . .

It would be a strange irony if the greatest of all early biblical scholars should also be the supreme example of one who taught hellenistic philosophy and called it Christianity.[11]

Here and there scattered through these volumes, are references to some very strange interpretations of the Bible, even by the greatest minds of Christendom. Thus, for example, no less a person than St. Augustine says that the six waterpots at the marriage in Cana of Galilee (Jn 2:6) represent the six ages of the world, from Adam to the last judgment. "And the sixth age begins with the coming of the Lord who conforms our mind to his own image and turns water into wine as a sign."[12] I am afraid that many have wrongly made the same confession as Dionysis of Alexandria, who, writing about 250 A.D. on the subject of the book of Revelation, confessed that he couldn't pretend to understand it and it should be interpreted allegorically.[13]

Early in the beginning of volume 2 is a very important statement regarding a matter I had not seen before. As all students will admit there has always been more or less of a mystery surrounding the Abisha scroll of the Samaritan

Pentateuch located at Nablus. The Samaritans themselves claim that the manuscript was pre-Christian. Now, since photographs of the scroll have been published with an editing of the text (1959), "The scroll, far from being a pre-Christian text, is merely a collection of medieval texts, written by Amisha ben Pinhas in 1085. Consequently the actual text of the Samaritan Pentateuch cannot claim antiquity except by implication. . . . It appears unlikely that in future an appeal to the Samaritan text will carry the same authority as previously."[14]

Though I had read considerably in the subject of Christ and art, I did not know that on the walls of the catacombs of Rome neither the crucifixion or resurrection are anywhere depicted, which has initiated a great deal of controversy. In fact, "no earlier representation is to be found than that carved on the wooden door of the church S. Sabina at Rome which was built about 430 A.D."[15]

The third volume of this remarkable *Cambridge History of the Bible* carries the subtitle, *The West from the Reformation to the Present Day.* Some material here, especially the two large sections on Continental versions, will not have much relevance for most of us, but there are some sections that are invaluable; for example, the two long sections on English versions from 1525 to the present day. There is a section, very rare for a work of this kind, on the "Bible and the Missionary," and then separate articles on the "Religion of Protestants" and "Bible in the Roman Catholic Church," and a long discussion on the "Criticism and Theological Use of the Bible, 1700-1950." It is not my purpose to inject criticisms of one kind or another, but only to indicate something of the contents of these rich pages. In the chapter on modern biblical scholarship there are some very interesting acknowledgments. Let me quote three of them:

Most theologians today seem to agree that the non-biblical category of 'inspiration' is not adequate to the elucidation of the doctrine of biblical revelation. . . . It is hardly an exaggeration to say that the psychology of religion has thrown no light on the mysterious processes by which the revelation of God is communicated to his prophets or by which the knowledge of God is born in the heart of the simple believer. . . .

There is a sense in which, though there is progress in scientific knowledge, there is not necessarily an equivalent progress in men's existential awareness of the personal being as standing over against, yet in the presence of, their Creator, who commands their obedience. . . . 'Progressive revelation' does not give us an adequate account of the knowledge of God as it is encountered in the scriptural writings.[16]

The last paragraph begins with this confession. "There is a general dissatisfaction in the mid-twentieth century with the liberal view of the authority of Scripture." There is a remarkable acknowledgment of the supremacy of the Scriptures over all other world literature by the distinguished apologete, Alan Richardson, when he says, "The Bible is different from all other books, even from the great Christian classics. It is eyewitness testimony to God's saving action in history; and therefore inevitably the canon of the Bible is closed when the sum total of the witness of the community which had known the apostles at first hand has been collected together."[17]

I have read this before but it is good to hear it reemphasized in this contemporary work that "The toughness of the indigenous churches would seem to depend on the degree of devotion to the Bible."[18] This chapter on the Bible and the Missionary begins with a refreshing statement.

The missionary, therefore, has been bound to the Bible by a threefold cord: his own spiritual life and his authority as a messenger of the Gospel depended on his own knowledge of the Scriptures; the message he sought to proclaim and the Church into which he brought his converts was centered on the Bible; and the written Scriptures were a means by which the Gospel could lay hold of the minds and hearts of men and women, sometimes more effectively than by any word of his own.[19]

Uniquely, at the end of this volume is an extensive bibliography of Aids to the Study of the Bible, in addition to bibliographies for all the various subjects which are discussed in these pages.

S. L. Greenslade, Regius Professor of Ecclesiastical History in the University of Oxford, was, fortunately, assigned to write the epilogue of this epochal work. Let me quote one passage:

Any attempt to measure the moral influence of the Bible would be presumptuous. We must be content to indicate some of the ways in which it has been at work, if possible without injustice to the moral teaching of Greece and Rome and of other civilizations. Some of its simplest lessons have been among the most far-reaching in effect, lessons which could have been learned from elsewhere, but were in fact taught to most western men by the Bible, either directly or indirectly in the simple moral instruction of the Church. Thou shalt do not murder, thou shalt not commit adultery, thou shalt not steal, thou shalt not bear false witness; speak the truth, hold to your word, help other people, look after the poor, the widow and the orphan—the simple elements of personal ethics on which a decent society depends—these are not specifically biblical, but they have been drummed into us through the Bible, and, despite St. Paul's excellent psychology in the seventh chapter of Romans ("I had not known coveting, except

the law had said, Thou shalt not covet"), there must have
been multitudes of beneficial moral decisions taken "because the Bible tells me to." That for centuries generation after generation of Europeans and Americans have
learned by heart the Commandments and the Beatitudes
and the Parable of the Good Samaritan is a major, though
incalculable, factor in their history. . . .

When every necessary qualification and admission has
been made, it remains surpassingly true that the Bible
has been the pre-eminent source of moral reform, individual and social, for the western world.[20]

Throughout this work of solid scholarship, occasionally
there flash forth, as we have tried to indicate, a confession of a genuine love for the Word of God, a recognition
of its absolute uniqueness, and its supremacy. Thus the
book closes with the following lines:

It is [God's] self-giving in revelation and redemption
which finds us in and through Christ, and shows us, and
lays upon us, the way of eternal truth and life. This is
the Gospel which the Bible prepetually proclaims. It is
to be found nowhere else. We rejoice in all truth, but to
Christian faith—and the Christian does not pretend to
dispense with faith—the Gospel is the measure of, the
key to, all truth. In the coronation of the British Sov-
ereign the Holy Bible is presented with these words:
"This Book, the most valuable thing that this world af-
fords. Here is Wisdom; This is the royal Law; These are
the lively Oracles of God."[21]

We are informed in the preface to this book that the
same publishing house is planning for a fourth volume devoted entirely to a history of the Bible in the English language, "more ample than any recent one . . . and further
volumes may take up other aspects of the story or cover
other areas."[22]

5

Preservation of What We Have Read

ONE OF THE MOST IMPORTANT DECISIONS which a minister must make is how is he going to keep the material which he thinks is worth preserving, that he may easily draw upon these resources, all that he has read and annotated. It is only a few rare people who can remember everything they have read, and I am assuming that this is not the kind of people to whom I am writing.

I have never been drawn to the use of large index volumes, in which are entered by alphabet or by number all clippings, book references, and so on. What we need is simplicity. I do not want to suggest something that involves a lot of red tape, or that becomes a master instead of a slave. What I am *suggesting* can be enlarged upon as the minister proceeds through life. Each man will have to develop details according to his own needs and disposition.

After all, it seems to me there are only four ways in which a person can make available through the years what he has studied and read. The first, and the least important probably, though frequently practiced by ministers, is to insert material in the margin of one's Bible. One of the earlier editions of the Scofield Bible had very wide margins, and had about forty ruled blank pages at the end. There are other similar editions of the Bible.

It would not be out of place, I think, to quote here a

letter which Alexander Whyte addressed to his nephew,
Hubert Simpson, about to begin his studies for the ministry, when Whyte himself was sixty-five years of age.

> Dear Hubert,—I send for your acceptance today an In-
> terleaved Study Bible. I have used such a Bible ever since
> I was at your state of study, and the use it has been to
> me is past all telling. For more than forty years, I think
> I can say, never a week, scarcely a day, has passed, that
> I have not entered some note or notes into my Bible: and,
> then, I never preach or speak in any way that I do not
> consult my Interleaved Bible. I never read a book with-
> out taking notes for preservation one way or other. And
> I never come in my reading on anything that sheds light
> on any passage of Scripture that I do not set the refer-
> ence down in my Bible over against the passage it illus-
> trates. And, as time has gone on, my Bible has become
> filled with illustrative and suggestive matter *of my own
> collecting;* and, therefore, sure to be suggestive and help-
> ful to me in my work. *All* true students have their own
> methods of collecting and husbanding the results of their
> reading. But an Interleaved Bible is specially suitable
> and repaying to a preacher. The Bible deserves all our
> labour and all our fidelity; and we are repaid with usury
> for all the student-like industry we lay out upon it. If you
> wish a talk, and have anything to ask me about this meth-
> od,—come and let us have a talk.
>
> Praying that you may be the most industrious, prayer-
> ful, and successful of ministers.[1]

The question arises, what should one insert in these
margins? Entries must be brief, I would think, and they
must be important. Each man will have to determine for
himself what he is going to write in the margins of his
Bible. Thus, for example, recognizing that Psalm 110 is
the Old Testament passage most frequently quoted in the
New Testament Scriptures, one will want to enter the New

84 *The Minister in His Study*

Testament references where this psalm is used, which are as follows: Direct quotations are found in Matthew 22:44; 26:64; Mark 12:36; 14:62; 16:19; Luke 20:42-43; 22:69; Acts 2:34-35, 5:31; 1 Corinthians 15:25. Indirect quotations are in Ephesians 1:20; Colossians 3:1; 1 Peter 3:22. The psalm, especially in its relationship to Melchizedek, interpenetrates the epistle to the Hebrews, 1:3, 13; 5:6, 10; 7:3, 11, 15, 17, 21, 24, 28; 8:1; 10:12-13; 12:2.

When studying the great promises of Genesis, I always repeat the remarkable words of the great German theologian, J. H. Kurtz, when commenting upon the opening verses of Genesis 12: "As the body is adapted and destined for the soul and the soul for the body, so is Israel for that country and that country for Israel. Without Israel the land is like a body from which the soul has fled; banished from its country, Israel is like a ghost which cannot find rest."[2]

I have always been fond of these words of Luther in his *Table Talk* regarding the inexhaustibleness of the Word of God.

> We must ever remain scholars here; we cannot sound the depth of one single verse in Scripture; we get hold but of the A B C and that imperfectly. . . .
>
> I have many times essayed thoroughly to investigate the ten commandments, but at the very outset, "I am the Lord thy God," I stuck fast; that very one word, I, put me to a *non-plus*. He that has but one word of God before him, and out of that word cannot make a sermon, can never be a preacher.[3]

On Luke's account of the episode of Dives and Lazarus, Whyte uttered one unforgettable sentence: "There is no pulpit anywhere with the concentrated terror of our Lord's pulpit when as here He takes us and lays our ears against the door of hell."[4]

John A. Scott, for many years professor of Greek literature at Northwestern University, and during his day probably the outstanding authority on Homer in our country, paid this splendid tribute to St. Luke:

> Luke was not only a Doctor and an historian, but he was one of the world's greatest men of letters. He wrote the clearest and the best Greek written in that century. . . .
>
> If Jesus had two human parents, why did the shrewd Gentile physician never suspect that fact? Since the arguments were sufficient to convince Dr. Luke, we know that we are dealing with no ignorant childish fancy.[5]

The American Bible Society has issued a wonderfully helpful New Testament with holes punched for binding that has a margin that measures 8½ by 10¾ inches, the one column of the text occupying 2½ inches. The rest of the page is left blank for notes, and one can put in these columns everything he intends to use in teaching any one book of the New Testament. The set extends to 615 pages.

The second type of classification of material is notebooks, and here there is room for a great variety of material. I suppose there are many ministers who have spent thirty years in the ministry without developing a single notebook.

There are two kinds of notebooks, of course. There is the ordinary stiff covered notebook such as is used in high school and college which can be purchased new for forty or fifty cents, with pagination varying from 150 to 300. Then there are the large clothbound record notebooks of various sizes, some of which are 8 by 10 inches, some 8 by 12 inches, or even 8½ by 14 inches with pagination extending from 150 to 500 pages. These are rather expensive, but you do not need many within a period of ten years; and they are worth what they cost. For myself I have always

used the cheaper notebooks for secondary studies, or preliminary bibliographies, but whenever I began to develop
a major subject, that is, major in my own life (and there
are many great subjects one 'cannot master), I would in-
variably use a large clothbound National 300-page Record
book. Of course, everyone must adapt this business of
notebooks to his needs and interests. Hundreds of ministers will not be teaching in theological seminaries, but it
so happened that some of us have had this privilege. In
my course on the New Testament teaching regarding the
Holy Spirit, for example, I first developed a table of contents, inscribed this at the beginning of a large notebook,
and then assigned pages for each of the thirty subheadings.
You can keep on adding to a notebook like this for years.
Sometimes, I am sorry to say I have begun notebooks on
some great subject and never got beyond the twentieth
page, for one reason or another. One could also have a
notebook in which he simply copies sentences or paragraphs or pages which he wants to keep, a miscellaneous
notebook. One might even have a notebook devoted to
one's own thinking regarding a certain area of Scripture or
of some great theme. I once began a notebook about what
the Bible says about the Word of God, without consulting
any other book or commentary, and I still remember what
precious things the Lord sent into my mind as I meditated
upon the power of the Word of God in creation.

The value of the minister's carefully kept notebooks is
well estimated by Herrick Johnson:

> Books that should *grow* in the ideal study—a scrap-
> book, a commonplace book, a text-book, a lecture-room-
> talk book, and a record book. These five books cannot be
> found at the bookstore. No money can buy them. They
> are products of experience; records of work done and to

be done; in a sense, personal histories and prophecies. They cannot be made to order. They are growths. They are blank-books when a minister begins with them. They will become bank-books, before he is through with them, with ever-increasing balance to his credit upon which he can draw at will, if they have been kept with any kind of discriminating care.[6]

In the third place, if a person is inclined at all to clip magazines and newspapers, he will want some kind of a filing system. For the minister there seems to be only three classifications. One is alphabetical, one is by subject, and one is by text. The alphabetical file is a very simple one to construct. A young pastor may want to begin this in an elementary way, and purchase a set of file folders broken up into the alphabet of our language. This is an inexpensive item. Later, he may want to divide this into certain sections, as for instance, for the word *Christ* one might have separate folders as the Names of Christ, Life of Christ, Teachings of Christ, Death of Christ et cetera. Then in this alphabetical file, there might be names of cities. They could be biblical cities, or famous cities of Europe which he wishes to visit or about which he wishes to gather material as Venice, Geneva, Paris, and London. Different men will be interested in different subjects.

The textual file is a simple matter. A pastor could get a series of file folders on which he would inscribe the various books of the Bible, sometimes combining several books into one folder, such as the three epistles of John.

Then there is what is known as a subject classification which can be quite complicated. The most famous classification by subject is that known as the Dewey Decimal System.[7] This is divided into ten major divisions as follows:

General Works   Pure Science
Philosophy   Applied Science
Religion   Arts and Recreation
Social Sciences   Literature
Linguistics   History

Each of these major subjects is divided into nine minor subject headings. No pastor, of course, will use all of these one hundred headings, but he might use thirty or forty of them. The subject of Religion is divided as follows:

Natural theology
Bible
Systematic or Doctrinal Theology
Devotional Theology
Pastoral Theology
Ecclesiastical Theology
Christian Church History
Christian Churches and Sects
Non-Christian Religions

This classification of religion has been extensively developed, both in the Dewey Catalog, and in various other bibliographic works. Every minister will want to construct his own details for such material. I would not be a slave to any system that someone else has developed. Let there be a lot of freedom in this. You don't want to get lost in your own filing system. All this material is just for your help, not to be passed upon in any examination for librarianship.

The most important filing scheme for a minister of the Word of God, I have left for the last, and this is the matter of a card index. Card indexes for the minister are of two kinds, textual and alphabetical. The textual cards will develop as the years come and go. On them you generally put references to relevant literature which for the most part will be of a sermonic nature, but sometimes you will want to copy on cards something you have found unusually rich, or pages in a theological work relating to some particular passage in the Word of God or period of church history. I can only speak for myself here. I have a four-fold card index. One is by text, one is alphabetical, a third is what I call an index to the Bible in Life and Literature, in which I have material that I have placed on yellow cards. Then I have a complete index to the International Sunday School Lessons from 1875 down to the present time. It would be an excellent index for any minister to have, not just one who is writing on the Sunday school lesson.

Let me illustrate what I mean. I have begun recently a series of messages on Romans 8 and I turned at once to my files to see what I had. Surprisingly enough, inasmuch as this is one of the greatest chapters of the Bible, I find that the international lesson system has had only one lesson, in 1903, devoted to Romans 8:1-14 in nearly one hundred years. On Romans 8:10-17, there have been two lessons in that period in 1935 and 1966. In 1960 there was one lesson devoted to the entire eighth chapter. So I would think that the material from the International Lessons would not be called important.

The first card that I turned up in my own files was on Romans 8 itself. It is in three handwritings, an earlier writing of my own which was quite clear, some lines by a secretary, and some more recent notes in my less legible handwriting. I discovered from this card the following five volumes devoted exclusively to an exposition of this chap ter:

John R. Macduff, *St. Paul's Song of Songs*
Marcus Rainsford, *No Condemnation, No Separation*
Octavius Winslow, *No Condemnation in Christ Jesus*

Alexander Hamilton, *Romans VIII*
J. Oswald Dykes, *The Gospel According to St. Paul*

Actually, in my file for Romans 8, I found sixty-two cards, of which thirty-seven had references to sermonic literature, some of them quite extensive. For example, on Romans 8:9 I have the following references:

> G. Campbell Morgan, *The Westminster Pulpit*, vol.
> 4, pp. 97-104
> ———, *The Christian World Pulpit*, vol. 59, pp. 377-79
> A. J. Gossip, *The Galilean Accent*, pp. 1 ff.
> H. C. G. Moule, *Veni Creator*, pp. 29 ff.
> Charles H. Spurgeon, *Metropolitan Tabernacle Pulpit*, vol. 19, no. 1133.

The question that arises is Where are you going to get these references to these sermons on Romans 8? One source, of course, is the sermonic material that you possess in your own library, and the quicker you index all of this material the easier it will be to discover what sermonic material you may have on any given text. Then, of course, you may turn to bibliographies, in such works as the *Great Texts of the Bible* or *The Speaker's Bible*. These are British works, and, excellent as they are, they contain hundreds of references to volumes that the ordinary minister will never see. To be frank, many are not in any library in this country. There is no need to index all this. Take the matter of Spurgeon's great *Metropolitan Tabernacle Pulpit*. I happen to have a complete set and a printed index to the entire series, so I have put on cards all the references to Romans 8. In Spurgeon's series of sermons, there are thirty-one. But if a man does not have this set of Spurgeon, or if he does not have access to such a series, what is the use of indexing sermons on any given text from Spurgeon?

Perhaps a minister is near a good theological library where he will find hundreds of volumes of sermons. If so, he will want to take advantage of the material available. For example, the library at the Moody Bible Institute of Chicago has a fairly complete index by Scripture texts to their hundreds of volumes of sermons, and I believe there is a similar index in the library of the Western Theological Seminary in Pittsburg.

May I frankly express myself here in saying that there are a lot of trivial volumes of sermons published in every decade. It is only a waste of time to index them, and a greater waste of time reading them. If I were a young minister, I would collect only the very best sermons by Spurgeon, G. Campbell Morgan, Alexander Maclaren, Hugh Macmillan, H. P. Liddon, W. M. Clow, James Stewart, Martyn Lloyd-Jones, and Joseph Parker, and those in the invaluable annual publication, *Keswick Week*. Some of the older magazines had excellent sermonic material such as the *British Weekly*, *The Homiletic Review*, and the *Record of Christian Work*.

Only this last week did I find something of great value to put on one of these index cards. It is the statement of Sir Martin Ryle that appeared in the new periodical *World*: "My own belief is that there can be no final answer to how the universe began. The question is, perhaps, too big to be answered."[8] Surely one wants to keep a statement like this on a card that would probably be headed "The Origin of the Universe Unknown."

Before turning to another subject, let me refer to a very simple matter which, nevertheless, needs careful attention, and that is, what to do with parallel passages in the gospels. The story of the five thousand is found in Matthew 14:15-21; Mark 6:32-44; Luke 9:12-17; and John 6:1-14. If one is preaching on any one of these passages—for ex-

ample, the one in Matthew—he should remember when
looking up sermons on this paragraph that he probably will
also find equally relevant material indexed under one of
the other three gospels. This problem does not occur outside of sermonic material in relation to the gospels, and
often, of course, many passages in the gospels are unique
and solitary—for example, most of the nativity narrative
of Luke and most of the great discourses of Jesus delivered
during His Perean ministry, as well as most of the passages
recording the events of Thursday of Holy Week in the dis-
course of Christ to His disciples, John 13-17.

We have considered briefly the four major methods for
preserving material that some day we may want to consult
or use, namely, wide margin or interleaved Bibles, notebooks of one kind or another, file folders (alphabetical or
by subject), and card indexes. I cannot close this discussion without referring to an unusual method of indexing sermons, which probably none of you have ever seen.

When I became edtior of *Peloubet's Notes on the International Lesson,* I acquired from the estate of the former
editor, Amos R. Wells, not only some hundreds of volumes
but also his own personal notebook index to sermons. This
is arranged in the order of the books of the Bible, and by
chapters and verse for each book. Thus, for example, on
Romans 8:28, Wells indexed nine sermons, of which let
me refer to four. This is the order in which they appear:

308	641	851	929
77	201	42	215

The upper figure refers to the book itself and the lower
figure to the page of that book in which the sermon begins.
At the end of the notebook is his list of sermon volumes
identified by numbers, not in alphabetical order but just
as Wells had time to index them. There are 1,715 books

of sermons indexed, which I would estimate represents
about 20,000 sermons, all indexed in one single volume.
Some of them are obscure, of which no one ever heard of
today; but some of them are tremendously important. For
example, the four books I have just listed above, are as follows: Burrell, *Old Time Religion;* Warfield, *Faith and Life;*
Taylor, *Hopefulness;* Batchelor, *Incarnation.* Wells rarely
gave the initials for the authors he listed.

While we are on this subject of indexing, may I suggest
that there are some volumes in one's library that I would
never think of indexing, as for instance, the thirty-two
volumes of Maclaren's *Expositions of Holy Scripture,*
where there must be about 1,200 sermons. Why index
these when in one minute one can determine by examin-
ing the relevant volume whether there is a particular sermon by Maclaren on the text in which one is interested.
The same is true of Joseph Parker's *The People's Bible* or
William B. Riley's now seldom seen *Bible of the Expositor
and the Evangelist* (forty volumes, published between
1924 and 1938), or even the often rich pages of *The Expositor's Bible.*

May I add here a word of warning. Many have developed the habit of making notes on the blank pages of a
volume they may be reading, indicating certain important
passages that we want to remember, but the trouble is that
over a period of several years we do not remember what
was written in the book. One, for instance, might be
reading a biography of Goethe and come upon some statement regarding Goethe's opposition to the cross of Christ.
This is interesting and important. One may even make
a note of it in the back of the volume, but when he has
finished with the volume he should transfer these notes
to his card index. There is nothing wrong with making
such notes, but they can only be made permanently avail-

able when the material is put on cards and filed away. Very often I come upon references in my card index, in my own handwriting, calling my attention to material read years ago that I had absolutely forgotten. If we are reading great literature embracing many important subjects, we will have this wealth of material available only when it is properly filed away where we can appropriate it within a few moments of time.

are twenty different titles listed by F. F. Bruce, eighteen by Leon Morris, nineteen by Stibbs, and fifteen by John Stott. I would call this an indispensable tool for the serious student.

Through the years it has been my privilege to publish a number of bibliographies; and perhaps it is here, for the first time, I should attempt to list the more important, in chronological order. In fact, my first publication was *A List of Bibliographies of Theological and Biblical Literature* (1931), long out of print. This subject was more exhaustively treated later (1955) in *A Bibliography of Bibliographies in Religion* by John G. Barrow. In 1939 appeared the first edition of *Profitable Bible Study*, which contained a classified, annotated list of over 150 books for the Bible student's library. Moody Press published (1948) my *Annotated Bibliography of D. L. Moody*, subsequently extensively used by many students writing theses for graduate degrees. Later I compiled "Recent Lives of Christ" for *His*, March 1950. In 1951 I published an extensive bibliography of important books for the Christian student in *His*, April 1951, which Inter-Varsity reprinted in separate form with the title, *Books to Put to Work*. That same year appeared my *Chats from a Minister's Library*, which contains chapters on various books but not strict bibliographies.

In 1952 Wilde published my *Preliminary Bibliography for the Study of Biblical Prophecy*, which needs thorough revision. In 1960 appeared *A Treasury of Books for Bible Study*, which contained chapter-length bibliographies: the history of preaching, the flora of the Bible, thanksgiving, the birth of Christ and Christmas, and the virgin Mary. In my *Biblical Doctrine of Heaven* is a bibliography something over 170 titles.

In the *Fuller Library Bulletin* for January-June 19...

Appendix 1:

About Bibliographies

A GREAT NUMBER of attempts have been made to construct bibliographies for the seminary student and active pastor. Probably the best, most comprehensive work, though it is now somewhat out-of-date, is *A Guide to Christian Reading*, published by the Inter-Varsity Fellowship of London. The first edition appeared in 1952, but a new edition, entirely revised, appeared in 1961. The material is carefully classified with occasional brief notations as to content.

The faculty of Princeton Theological Seminary has issued three important bibliographies: *A Bibliography of Bible Study for Theological Students*, first published in 1948 and thoroughly revised in 1960; *Bibliography of Practical Theology* in 1949; and *A Bibliography of Systematic Theology for Theological Students*, also in 1949. These are not to be reprinted or revised.

A helpful book is *Tools for Bible Study*, edited by B. H. Kelly and D. G. Miller, and published by the John Knox Press of Richmond in 1956. The Roman Catholics published an excellent work, *An Introductory Bibliography for the Study of Scripture*, by G. S. Glanzman and J. A. Fitzmeyer, and published by Newman Press, Westminster, Maryland in 1961. A worthwhile volume is *Using Theological Books and Libraries*, by Ella V. Aldrich and Thomas Edward Camp, and published by Prentice-Hall, New York, in 1963.

A scholarly, exhaustive work was published by Frederick W. Danker in 1960, *Multipurpose Tools for Bible Study* (Concordia xviii.289). This volume gives more attention to Continental works than any bibliography of its kind. Some theological seminaries are now issuing very important bibliographies, though a great deal of the older, still valuable titles regretfully are being passed by. The Southwestern Baptist Theological Seminary has just issued (1972) *Essential Books for Christian Ministry.* This includes about 1,000 titles arranged by subject.

The Union Theological Seminary of Richmond, Virginia, has now published the fourth edition (1968) of their *Essential Books for a Pastor's Library* in which are listed with some annotations, probably 850 titles. It is very significant that a tenth of the entire list is devoted to the subject of ethics.

The Theological Education Fund in 1960 published a large *Theological Book List* by Raymond P. Morris, a quarto-size work of 240 pages, with an index of over 3,300 authors. This list was put together by forty different scholars from America, Great Britain, and Europe.

I do not know how many will be interested in the literature concerning travels in Palestine; but for those who are, may I call attention to a volume not too well known, *Western Pilgrims,* published by the Franciscan Press of Jerusalem in 1952. This large quarto work, in addition to the reprinting of three famous itineraries of the fourteenth century, gives a list of works in English on the Holy Land numbering over 300 titles.

The Southwestern Baptist Theological Seminary of Fort Worth, Texas, has published *A Bibliography for Pastors and Theological Students,* which helpfully contains a list of theological journals.

Of course, the most famous list of books for the study

of the Scriptures is now almost one hundred years old, *Commenting and Commentaries,* by that superlative preacher, Charles H. Spurgeon, a work of something over 300 pages. Spurgeon includes about 3,000 titles, most of them with annotations. It was a remarkable piece of work for anyone preaching to such great audiences as Spurgeon whose sermons were published every week, and who continued for years to edit the *Sword and Trowel.* Some of the volumes in this bibliography are still valuable, while others do not justify consulting. There is only one major flaw in this extensive bibliography, and that is Spurgeon's strange aversion to the whole subject of biblical prophecy which was manifest in more ways than one. His flippant remarks about the interpretation of some of the prophecies in the book of Daniel and the book of Revelation were unworthy of these great portions of the Word of God.

The most recent important bibliography for ministers and Bible students has just been published by the Inter-Varsity Press (1971), *Encounter with Books,* edited by H. G. Marchant. Here is an excellently classified bibliography of some 1,600 volumes, all of them with excellent brief notes—a work that is the product of the cooperation of sixty-five contemporary evangelical scholars. In fact I doubt if any single scholar today, or even five of them, could have produced a work like this. The literature appraised from an evangelical viewpoint. Most of the books listed are of the twentieth century, and for that reason some of the major works of a former generation are regretfully not found here; for example, the great *Systematic Theology* of Charles Hodge and the writings of Alford do not appear here. The references to some of the men who have been identified closely with the work of the Inter-Varsity in Great Britain are more extensively is generally found in reference to other authors.

an extensive "Bibliography of the Influence of the Bible on English Literature," and in the issue of October 1953–September 1954 is the most complete study of its kind that has been attempted, "A Bibliography of Biblical, Ecclesiastical, and Theological Dictionaries and Encyclopaedias published in Great Britain and America."

Appendix 2:

A Further Word Regarding the New Testament with Fuller References

THE *New Testament with Fuller References* is a reprint of the Revised Version of 1881, with this tremendous apparatus of footnotes. Perhaps the principle involved stated at the beginning of the volume will indicate what here has been so successfully carried through.[1]

> A simple index letter is employed where there is an exact or close parallel between the passages. This very often indicates an identity of the Greek words. Where a phrase or a combination of words is the subject of the reference the index letter is repeated with each element.
>
> *Cited,* or *Cited from,* is prefixed to cases of actual quotation.
>
> *Cp.* (compare) is prefixed to references where the parallel is less exact, or the words are only partially identical. Sometimes *Cp.* indicates contrast; at other times an indirect allusion to a passage which is not distinctly cited.
>
> *See* is prefixed generally when reference is made to a parallel passage on which a body of references has been collected. Sometimes it is used for reference to longer passages, parallel or explanatory.
>
> References in thick type, in the Synoptic Gospels, indicate that substantial identity exists between passages found in different Gospels, or different parts of the same Gospel.

Perhaps we might illustrate this by the references assigned to Luke 8:28-30.

> 28. And when he saw Jesus, he ᵗcried out, and ᵘfell down before him, and ᵗwith a loud voice said, ᵛWhat have I to do with thee, Jesus, ʷthou Son of ˣthe Most High God? I beseech thee, torment me not. 29. For he commanded the ʸunclean spirit to come out from the man. For ¹oftentimes it had ᵃseized him: and he was kept under guard, and bound with chains and fetters; and breaking the bands asunder, he was driven of the ²devil into ᵇᶜthe deserts. 30. And Jesus asked him, What is thy name? And he said, ᵈLegion; for many ³devils were entered into him.

28. ᵗch. 4:33, 34; Mark 1:23, 26; Acts 8:7. ᵘver. 41, 47; ch. 5:8, 12; 17:16; Mark 3:11; 5:22, 33; 7:25; John 11:32. ᵛch. 4:34; Matthew 8:29; Mk. 1:24; Jn. 2:4; cp. 2 Ch. 35:21, Jg. 11:12; 2 S. 16:10; 19:22; 1 K. 17:18; 2 K. 3:13; 1 Esd. 1:26. ʷCp. ch. 4:3, 9; see Mt. 14:33. ˣch. 1:32; 6:35; Gn. 14:18-20, 22; Nu. 24:16; Ps. 57:2; 78:56; Is. 14:14; Dn. 3:26; 4:24, 32; 5:18, 21; 7:18, 22, 25, 27; 1 Esd. 6:31; Ac. 16:17; He. 7:1; cp. Is. 57:15; Mic. 6:6, Ac. 7:48, al.

¹Or, ᶻof a long time. ²Gr. demon. ³Gr. demons.

29. ʸSee Mk. 3:30. ᶻCp. ch. 20:9. ᵃAc. 6:12; 19:29. ᵇCp. ver. 27, Mark 5:5. ᶜCp. ch. 11:24; Mt. 12:43; see ch. 5:16.

30. ᵈMt. 26:53; Mk. 5:15.

Appendix 3:

Comments by Some Great Men of the Ministry on Books and Reading

RICHARD BAXTER, a self-taught preacher, acquired great learning through reading. A prolific writer as well as avid reader, he produced more than one hundred works. The following comments are taken from the twenty-three-volume *Practical Works of the Rev. Richard Baxter.*

RICHARD BAXTER ON BOOKS AND READING

THE VALUE OF BOOKS

Because God hath made the excellent, holy writings of his servants, the singular blessing of this land and age; and many an one may have a good book, even any day or hour of the week, that cannot at all have a good preacher; I advise all God's servants to be thankful for so great a mercy, and to make use of it, and be much in reading; for reading with most doth more conduce to knowledge than hearing doth, because you may choose what subjects and the most excellent treatises you please; and may be often at it, and may peruse again and again what you forget, and may take time as you go to fix it on your mind: and with very many it doth more than hearing also to move the heart, though hearing of itself, in this hath the advantage; because lively books may be more easily had, than lively preachers: especially these sorts of men should be much in reading. 1. Masters of families, that have more souls to care for than their own. 2. People that live where there is no preaching, or as bad or worse than none. 3. Poor people, and servants, and children, that are forced on many Lord's day to stay at home, whilst others have the opportunity to hear. 4. And vacant persons that have more leisure than others have.[1]

THE READING OF BOOKS

Question: What books, especially of theology, should one choose, who for want of money or time, can read but few?

Answer: General. The truth is, 1. It is not the reading of many books which is necessary to make a man wise or good; but the well reading of a few, could he be sure to have the best. 2. And it is not possible to read over very many on the same subjects, without a great deal of loss of precious time; 3. And yet the reading of as many as is possible tendeth much to the increase of knowledge, and were the best way, if greater matters were not that way unavoidably to be omitted: life therefore being short, and work great, and knowledge being for love and practice, and no man having leisure to learn all things, a wise man must be sure to lay hold on that which is most useful and necessary. 4. But some considerable acquaintance with many books is now become by accident necessary to a divine. 1. Because unhappily a young student knoweth not which are the best, till he hath tried them; and when he should take another man's word, he knoweth not whose word it is that he should take: for among grave men, accounted great scholars, it is few that are judicious and wise, and he that is not wise himself cannot know who else are so indeed: and every man will commend the authors that are of his own opinion. And if I commend to you some authors above others, what do I but commend my own judgment to you, even as if I commended my own books, and persuaded you to read them; when another man of a different judgment will commend to you

books of a different sort. And how knoweth a raw student
which of us is in the right? 2. Because no man is so full
and perfect as to say all that is said by all others; but
though one man excel in one or many respects, another
may excel him in some particulars, and say that which he
omitteth, or mistaketh in. 3. But especially because many
errors and adversaries have made many books necessary
to some, for to know what they say, and to know how to
confute them, especially the Papists, whose way is upon
pretence of antiquity and universality, to carry every
controversy into a wood of church-history, and ancient
writers, that there you may first be lost, and then they
may have the finding of you: and if you cannot answer
every corrupted or abused citation of their's out of councils and fathers, they triumph as if they had justified their
church-tyranny. 4. And the very subjects that are to be
understood are numerous, and few men write of all. 5.
And on the same subject men have several modes of writing; as one excelleth in accurate method, and another in
clear, convincing argumentation, and another in an affectionate, taking style: and the same book that doth one,
cannot well do the other, because the same style will not
do it.[2]

Vocal preaching hath the pre-eminence in moving the
affections, and being diversified according to the state of
the congregations which attend it: this way the milk
cometh warmest from the breast. But books have the advantage in many other respects: you may read an able
preacher, when you have but a mean one to hear. Every
congregation cannot hear the most judicious or powerful
preachers; but every single person may read the books
of the most powerful and judicious. Preachers may be
silenced or banished, when books may be at hand: books
may be kept at a smaller charge than preachers: we may
choose books which treat of that very subject which we
desire to hear of; but we cannot choose what subject the

preacher shall treat of. Books we may have at hand every day and hour; when we can have sermons but seldom, and at set times. If sermons be forgotten, they are gone. But a book we may read over and over until we remember it; and, if we forget it, may again peruse it at our pleasure, or at our leisure. So that good books are a very great mercy to the world. The Holy Ghost chose the way of writing, to preserve his doctrine and laws to the church, as knowing how easy and sure a way it is of keeping it safe to all generations, in comparison of mere verbal tradition, which might have made as many controversies about the very terms, as there be memories or persons to be the preservers and reporters.

Books are (if well chosen) domestic, present, constant, judicious, pertinent, yea, and powerful sermons: and always of very great use to your salvation: but especially when vocal preaching faileth, and preachers are ignorant, ungodly, or dull, or when they are persecuted, and forbid to preach.

You have need of a judicious teacher at hand, to direct you what books to use or to refuse. For among good books there are some very good that are sound and lively: and some are good, but mean, and weak, and somewhat dull: and some are very good in part, but have mixtures of error, or else of incautious, injudicious expressions, fitter to puzzle than edify the weak. I am loath to name any of these latter sorts (of which abundance have come forth of late).[3]

Charles Bridges on the Use of Time for Study

In his famous work, *The Christian Ministry*, Charles Bridges had some sensible suggestions about the minister's use of time.

> Mr. Alleine would often say, "Give me a Christian that counts his time more precious than gold." Mr. Cotton would express his regret after the departure of a visitor—

"I had rather have given this man a handful of money, than have been kept thus long out of my study." Melancthon, when he had an appointment, expected, not only the hour, but the minute to be fixed, that time might not run out in the idleness of suspense. Seneca has long since taught us, that time is the only thing of which "it is a virtue to be covetous." But here we should be, like the miser with his money—saving it with care, and spending it with caution. It is well to have a book for every spare hour, to improve what Boyle calls the "parenthesis or interludes of time: which, coming between more important engagements, are wont to be lost by most men for want of a value for them: and even by good men, for want of skill to preserve them. And since goldsmiths and refiners"—he remarks—"are wont all the year long to save the very sweepings of their shops, because they may contain in them some filings or dust of those richer metals, gold and silver; I see not, why a Christian may not be as careful, not to lose the fragments and lesser intervals of a thing incomparably more percious than any metal—time; especially when the improvement of them by our meletetics may not only redeem so many portions of our life, but turn them to pious uses, and particularly to the great advantage of devotion."[4]

R. W. DALE ON A MINISTER'S READING

R. W. Dale, in his great series of lectures, *Nine Lectures on Preaching*, devoted two out of nine lectures to the subject of reading (pp. 63-115).

Gentlemen, it is four and twenty years since I left college, and the temptations to desultoriness which I have either yielded to or mastered would enable me to go on for four and twenty hours with the story of the perils which will beset you as soon as you leave these walls. You will be ruined, your own hopes and the hopes of your friends will all be blighted, unless you resolve, with God's help, to stand firm and to work as hard when you become a minister as you have worked while at the university.[5]

I assume that while you are here you will get a general view of the scheme of orthodox evangelical theology. You will carry away in your mind what may be called an index map of the whole territory of ascertained theological truth, as that territory is laid down by evangelical theologians of recognised authority. You will have learnt how they define the principal doctrines of their creed, the relations which they conceive to exist between these doctrines, and the general nature of the evidence by which it is supposed that the truth of the doctrines is demonstrated. If when you are beginning to preach you discover that here and there the lines of the map are beginning to fade, that perhaps great breadths of country have vanished altogether, so that you can give no account of them, I think you will do wise to recover your knowledge as soon as you are able. Whether you accept the whole scheme or not, you ought to be in complete possession of it.[6]

In preparing, two or three years ago, a series of lectures on the Atonement, I was able to save myself a large amount of labour by using notes of this kind which I had written sixteen or seventeen years before. If as you read you discuss in your notes the author's arguments and criticise his theories, you will obtain at the time a more complete mastery of his position, and your notes will be more useful to you afterwards.[7]

NOTES BY JOHN A. HUTTON

These notes were given during a series of lectures to divinity students in Aberdeen, Edinburgh, and Glasgow in the spring of 1921.

IN REGARD TO READING

To return to reading. As a general observation, I should say, don't read very much with the direct and immediate view to preaching. Read to make an able and wise man of yourself, conversant with life discerned spiritually as life is discerned spiritually in history and philosophy and art including poetry. You see we men of the Reformed Church, and of the Reformed Church over which a Puritan east wind blew for long, have to create our atmosphere. We do not preach in Cathedrals. We are therefore to carry our Cathedral about with us, so to speak. And what is the grace of a Cathedral but just this—it speaks to us of the test of time, of beauty also, and of a day in the history of the human soul when men were sure of God. All that we must somehow bring in spirit with us, or we must be able to invoke it.[8]

Resist the itch to read little passing books.

Avoid all "Aids to Preachers" so-called; that is the broad road that leadeth to commonplaceness and tediousness.

Save up, if need be, from all those passing feckless books, enough to buy, if you will, one book by some real scholar or master. I myself have always on hand some book which is really beyond me. It has the effect in the mind, to say no more, that the use of dumb-bells has on the muscles. It keeps one humble too: and when we lose humility, all is over with us.

Never read without taking notes: all other reading is self-indulgence and an occasion for sleep.[9]

My friend Dr. Leckie said nearly all that is to be said about reading to those who have ears to hear: Read what you like. That is to say, be a reading man. Then, Read what you don't like. And then, Read what you ought to like.[10]

A WORD CONCERNING THE HOURS OF STUDY

If we decide that we need to read three hours each day, taking notes all the time, then three hours let it be. If, on some particular day, the three hours are necessarily reduced, we would do well to make a note of the loss of time, and refuse to give our conscience its discharge until we have made up that lost time. For the one thing a man must fight for tooth and nail is that he shall be master of his circumstances; that he shall do with his time what he has decided he must in honour do.[11]

Well now in the case of such a man, if the day is to begin well it must begin the night before. The mood in which we rise in the morning depends a good deal upon the circumstances in which we lay down. It is an excellent plan to *note* on a piece of paper and to lay on your desk at night, what you propose to do and what, if God spares you, you shall do next day.[12]

A LIST OF HELPFUL BOOKS SUGGESTED BY H. C. G. MOULE

It is significant how out-of-date a list of helpful books for the minister can become. The following list of ten books is from *To My Younger Brethren* by H. C. G. Moule.

[I] have elsewhere called attention to the following among works helpful at present in the controversy about Scripture: Lord Hatherley's *Continuity of Scripture*, Dr. Waller's *Authoritative Inspiration*, Dr. Cave's *Inspiration of the Old Testament*. Let me add four able popular tractates: Cave's *Battle of the Standpoints* (Queen's Printers), Eckersley's *Historical Value of the Old Testament* (Society for Promoting Christian Knowledge), G. Carlyle's *Moses and the Prophets* and Seaver's *Authority of Christ* (Elliot Stock). Dr. Liddon's memorable sermon, *The Worth of the Old Testament*, is full of helpful suggestions. See too Professor Leathes' *Witness of the Old*

Testament to Christ, Sir J. W. Dawson's *Modern Science in Bible Lands,* and Bishop Harold Browne's *Messiah Foretold.* I specially call attention to Canon R. Girdlestone's recent book, the work of a master, *The Foundations of the Bible,* most temperate, judicial, solid, and establishing; and to this must be added now (1892) Bishop Ellicott's excellent Charge, published by the S.P.C.K. under the title *Christus Comprobator.*

Of all these books I think none of them would appear in a bibliography of today.

W. ROBERTSON NICOLL ON THE ADVANTAGE OF
REREADING

Scottish theologian, preacher, and editor Sir William Robertson Nicoll was well known as a literary critic. He felt that great books should be reread for increasing benefit.

The first advantage of rereading is that it gives one the true possession of a book. Most memories are exceedingly treacherous. Even when the memory is strong in certain directions, it is apt to be weak in others. A powerful verbal memory—the memory by which a man recollects a list of names or learns to repeat a string of verses—is not usually associated with the most serviceable memory of all: the memory which makes a man aware of his own knowledge, or at least the sources from which he can at any time draw inspiration.[14]

The memory is refreshed by the vision he loves, and the heart is refreshed with it. It is so with rereading. We know the book, but we discover that we do not know it, and that it has fresh felicities and delights disclosing themselves at each perusal. Besides, though the book does not change while it awaits us on the shelf, we keep changing. We bring more experience, more knowledge, more power of appreciation. (I am talking, of course, about the great books.) Suppose a man visits the Alps for the first time, and is ignorant of botany. He goes back another time, and during the interval he has learned to botanise. That will make a great difference. To compare Dr. Hort's letters on his Alpine journeys with those of the ordinary traveller is instructive. So it is with books. The pages are held to the fire of experience, and the living letters disclose themselves. When we know, not merely by reading or by imagining, what a great phase of life may mean either in joy or in sorrow, we discover new messages and new meanings in familiar pages. Even a small experience adds to the significance of our reading.[15]

I have read Boswell through on successive days at least twenty times.[16]

AUSTIN PHELPS ON THE MINISTER AND HIS STUDY

Congregational clergyman and author of many books on preaching, Austin Phelps was president of Andover Theological Seminary from 1869 to 1879. He expressed strong views on the effects of books upon a pastor's ministry.

This view suggests a third object of a pastor's study of books; viz., *assimilation* to the genius of the best authors. There is an influence exerted by books upon the mind which resembles that of diet upon the body. A studious mind becomes, by a law of its being, like the object which it studies with enthusiasm. If your favorite authors are superficial, gaudy, short-lived, you become yourself such in your culture and your influence. If your favorite authors are of the grand, profound, enduring order, you become yourself such to the extent of your innate capacity for such growth. Their thoughts become yours, not by transfer, but by transfusion. Their methods of combining thoughts become yours; so that, on different subjects from theirs, you will compose as they would have done if they had handled those subjects. Their choice of words, their idioms, their constructions, their illustrative materials, become yours; so that their style and yours will belong to the same class in expression, and yet your style will never be merely imitative of theirs.[17]

What, then, should be the influence of this impossibility of universal scholarship upon our literary plans? I answer in three particulars. One effect of it should be to prevent our wasting ourselves in impracticable plans of study. Every young man should take the measure of his time, his physical health, his degree of independence of other avocations, and specially his power of mental appropriation. Then his plans of reading should be adjusted accordingly. No other one habit is so unproductive to a student as that of omnivorous reading. The space which such a reader traverses in libraries is no evidence of his culture. The most useless men living are the bookworms who are nothing more. There are men who devour books because they are books. They read as if they fancied that the mechanical process of trotting doggedly through libraries were the great business of a life of culture. Such men can not possess sound learning.[18]

In a letter on the studies of a clergyman, he [Dr. Thomas Arnold of Rugby] expresses himself as follows; viz., "I would entreat every man with whom I had any influence, that, if he reads at all, he should read widely and comprehensively; that he should not read exclusively what is called divinity. Learning of this sort, when not mixed with that comprehensive study which alone deserves the name, is, I am satisfied, an actual mischief to a man's mind. It impairs his simple common sense. It makes him narrow-minded, and fills him with absurdities. If a man values power of seeing truth, and judging soundly, let him not read exclusively those who are called divines. With regard to the fathers, in all cases preserve the proportions of your reading. Read, along with the fathers, the writings of men of other times and of different powers of mind. Keep your view of men and things extensive. He who reads deeply in one class of writers only, gets views which are sure to be perverted, and which are not only narrow, but false. If I have a confident opinion on any one point connected with the improvement of the human mind, it is on this."[19]

It is frankly conceded, as has been already remarked in the preface to this volume, that any scholarly plan of study must, to the majority of pastors, be, to a greater or less extent, an *ideal* one. The practicability of it is a matter of degrees, exceedingly variable at different times, as well as to different persons. The ideal element must enter largely into any plan that shall be largely useful. If there are any to whom it can be only an ideal, it is not therefore useless, even to them. The *negative* value of a lofty ideal of scholarly life is not to be despised. It may act as a censor of a preacher's sermons, keeping alive a taste which will exclude unscholarly methods and material which he knows to be such, but which he will not avoid, except through a silent respect for his dumb library. The very sight of a library of a thousand volumes well chosen is a stimulus to a pastor who for months may not be able to read a volume. Says Bishop Hall on "The Sight of a Great Library," "Neither can I cast my eye casually on any of these silent masters but I must learn somewhat."[20]

Some Notes from Charles H. Spurgeon

ON COMMENTING AND COMMENTARIES

Probably the most widely used bibliography of commentaries on the Scriptures is the one which Spurgeon found time to compile in his busy life. There are about 3,000 volumes listed in this unique annotated bibliography. The weakest part of all of it is in relation to books on the prophets and Revelation. He practically admits this himself.

The writers on the Prophetical Books have completely mastered us, and after almost completing a full list, we could not in our conscience believe that a tithe of them would yield anything to the student but bewilderment, and therefore we reduce the number to small dimensions. We reverence the teaching of the prophets, and the Apocalypse, but for many of the professed expounders of those inspired books we entertain another feeling.[21]

If I can save a poor man from spending his money for that which is not bread, or, by directing a brother to a good book, may enable him to dig deeper into the mines of truth, I shall be well repaid. For this purpose I have toiled, and read much, and passed under review some three or four thousand volumes. From these I have compiled my catalogue, rejecting many, yet making a very varied selection.[22]

In order to be able to expound the Scriptures, and as an aid to your pulpit studies, you will need to be familiar with the commentators: a glorious army, let me tell you, whose acquaintance will be your delight and profit. Of course, you are not such wiseacres as to think or say that you can expound Scripture without assistance from the works of divines and learned men who have labored before you in the field of exposition. If you are of that opinion, pray remain so, for you are not worth the trouble of conversion, and like a little coterie who think with you, would resent the attempt as an insult to your infallibility. It seems odd, that certain men who talk so much of what the Holy Spirit reveals to themselves, should think so little of what he has revealed to others. My chat this afternoon is not for these great originals, but for you who are content to learn of holy men, taught of God, and mighty in the Scriptures.[23]

ON 2 TIMOTHY 4:13

Even an apostle must read. Some of our very ultra-
Calvinistic brethren think that a minister who reads books
and studies his sermon must be a very deplorable speci-
men of a preacher. A man who comes up into the pulpit,
professes to take his text on the spot, and talks any quan-
tity of nonsense, is the idol of many. If he will speak
without premeditation, or pretend to do so, and never
produce what they call a dish of dead men's brains—oh!
that is the preacher. How rebuked are they by the apostle! He is inspired, and yet he wants books! He has been
preaching at least for thirty years, and yet he wants
books! He has seen the Lord, and yet he wants books!
He had had a wider experience than most men, and yet
he wants books! He had been caught up into the third
heaven, and had heard things which it was unlawful for
a man to utter, yet he wants books! He had written the
major part of the New Testament, and yet he wants
books! The apostle says to Timothy and so he says to
every preacher, "Give thyself unto reading." The man
who never reads will never be read; he who never quotes
will never be quoted. He who will not use the thoughts
of other men's brains, proves that he has no brains of his
own. Brethren, what is true of ministers is true of all our
people. *You* need to read. Renounce as much as you will
all light literature, but study as much as possible sound
theological works, especially the Puritanic writers, and expositions of the Bible. We are quite persuaded that the
very best way for you to be spending your leisure, is to be
either reading or praying. You may get much instruction
from books which afterwards you may use as a true
weapon in your Lord and Master's service. Paul cried,
"Bring the books"—join in the cry.[24]

BOOKS RECOMMENDED BY JOHN WESLEY

John Wesley took a great deal of interest in the three

children of his brother Charles. To the daughter, Sarah, then about age twenty-one, he wrote this letter of advice. It seems that she took his advice to heart, for she became a well-informed woman and the friend to a distinguished literary circle.

Bristol, September 4, 1781

My dear Sally,—It is certain the Author of our nature designed that we should not destroy, but regulate, our desire for knowledge. What course you may take in order to this, I will now briefly point out.

1. You want to know God, in order to enjoy Him in time and eternity.

2. All you want to know of Him is contained in one book, the Bible. And all that you learn is to be referred to this, either directly or remotely.

3. Would it not be well, then, to spend, at least, an hour a day in reading and meditating on the Bible? reading, every morning and evening, a portion of the Old and New Testament, with the Explanatory Notes?

4. Might you not read two or three hours in the morning, and one or two in the afternoon? When you are tired of severer studies, you may relax your mind by history or poetry.

5. The first thing you should understand a little of is grammar. You may read first Kingswood English Grammar, and then Bishop Lowth's Introduction.

6. You should acquire, if you have not already, some knowledge of arithmetic. Dilworth's Arithmetic would suffice.

7. For geography, I think you need only read over Randal's or Guthrie's Geographical Grammar.

8. Watts' Logic is not a very good one; but I believe you cannot find a better.

9. In natural philosophy, you have all that y￰   ￰ to know in the "Survey of the Wisdom of God￰   n."

But you may add the Glasgow abridgment of Mr. Hutchinson's works.

10. With any, or all, of the foregoing studies, you may intermix that of history. You may begin with Rollin's Ancient History; and afterwards read, in order, the Concise History of the Church, Burnet's History of the Reformation, the Concise History of England, Clarendon's History of the Rebellion, Neal's History of the Puritans, his History of New England, and Robertson's History of America.

11. In metaphysics, you may read Locke's Essay on the Human Understanding, and Malebranche's Search after Truth.

12. For poetry, you may read Spenser's Fairy Queen, and select parts of Shakspeare, Fairfax, or Hoole; Godfrey of Bouillon, Paradise Lost, the Night Thoughts, and Young's Moral and Sacred Poems.

13. You may begin and end with divinity; in which I will only add, to the books mentioned before, Bishop Pearson on the Creed, and the Christian Library. By this course of study, you may gain all the knowledge which any reasonable Christian needs. But remember, before all, in all, and above all, your great point is, to know the only true God, and Jesus Christ whom He hath sent.

I am, my dear Sally, your affectionate uncle,

John Wesley.[25]

George Whitefield's List of Major Divinity Volumes

It is interesting to note how so many books recommended to theological students two hundred years ago, and even one hundred years ago, are no longer considered of basic value for the contemporary student of theology. In fact, many of these would be very difficult to find except in the larger theological libraries. In 1770 George Whitefield in his Rules for his Academy listed the following twenty-three volumes, or twenty-three authors actually.

> The following divinity books to be read: The Commentaries of Henry, Doddridge, Guise, Burkit, and Clarke; Wilson's Dictionary, Professor Francke's Manuductio, Doddridge's Rise and Progress, Boston's Fourfold State, and his Book on the Covenant, Jenks on the Righteousness of Christ, and also his Meditations, Hervey's Theron and Aspasio, Hall's Contemplations, and other works, Edwards's Preacher, Trapp on the Old and New Testament, Poole's Annotations, Warner's Tracts, Leighton's Comment on the First Epistle of Peter, Pearson's on the Creed, Edwards' Veritas Redux, and Owen and Bunyan's Works.[26]

Of these twenty-three authors the only ones that are even heard of today are Matthew Henry, Leighton on the First Epistle of Peter, the great work of Pearson on the Apostle's Creed, and, of course, the works of John Bunyan. Of these four, only one remains in many editions and about which books are continually appearing and that would be the works of John Bunyan, especially his *Pilgrim's Progress.*

ALEXANDER WHYTE ON THE MINISTER'S READING

In spite of his many responsibilities as minister of the largest and most influential church of the Free Church of Scotland—Free St. George's of Edinburgh, where he spent thirty-nine years—Alexander Whyte was a voluminous writer. Later as professor and then principal of New College, he stressed the importance of reading to his students.

> Every man who has read Paul's Epistles with the eyes of his understanding in light, and with his heart on fire, must have continually exclaimed, What a gift to a man is a fine mind, and that mind wholly given up to Jesus

Christ! Let our finest minds, then, devote themselves to the study of Christology. Other subjects may, or may not, be exhausted; other callings may, or may not, be over-crowded; but there is plenty of room in the topmost calling of all, and there is an ever-opening and ever-deepening interest there. No wonder, then, that it has been a University tradition in Scotland that our finest minds have all along entered the Divinity Hall. The other walks and callings of human life both need, and will reward, the best minds that can be spared to them, but let the service of our Lord and Saviour Jesus Christ first be filled. To annotate the Iliad, or the Symposium, or the Commedia; to build up and administer an empire; to command in a battle for freedom by sea or by land; to create and bequeath a great and enriching business; to conduct an influential newspaper; to be the rector of a great school, and so on,—these are all great services done to our generation when we have the talent, and the character, and the opportunity, to do them. But to master Paul, as Paul mastered Moses and Christ; to annotate, and illustrate, and bring freshly home to ten thousand readers, the Galatians, or the Romans, or the Colossians; to have eyes to see what Israel ought to do, and to have the patience, and the courage, to lead a great church to do it; to feed, and to feed better and better for a lifetime, the mind and the heart of a congregation of God's people, and then to depart to be with Christ,—let the finest minds and the deepest and richest hearts in every new generation fall down while they are yet young and say, Lord Jesus, what wilt Thou have me to do with my life, and with whatsoever talents Thou hast intrusted to me?[27]

. . . You are not eternally fore-ordained, indeed, to write the Epistle to the Romans, or the Epistle to the Ephesians. But you are chosen, and called, and matriculated, to do the next best thing to that. You are called to master those masterpieces of Paul, so as to live experi-

mentally upon them all your student life, and then you
are to teach and preach them to your people better and
better all your pulpit and pastoral life. You are to work
with your hands, if need be; you are to sell your bed, if
need be, as Coleridge commands you, in order to buy
Calvin on the Romans, and Luther on the Galatians, and
Goodwin on the Ephesians, and Davenant on the Colossians, and Hooker on Justification, and "that last word on
the subject," Marshall's *Gospel Mystery of Sanctification;*
and you are to husband-up your priceless and irrecovera-
ble hours to such studies, as you shall give account at the
day of divinity student's judgment. You are to feed your
people, when you have got them committed of Christ to
your charge, with the finest of the wheat, and with honey
out of the rock. And that, better and better all your life,
till your proud people shall make their boast in God about
you, as the proud people of Anwoth made their boast
about that great genius, and great scholar, and great theologian, and great preacher, and great pastor, Master Samuel Rutherford.[28]

    . . . Up, and abolish death. Up, out of your bondage
all your days through fear of death. Up, and practise dying in the Lord, till you take the prize. Up, and read Paul
without ceasing, and pray without ceasing, till you also
shall stand on tiptoe with expectation and with full assur-
ance of faith. Yes; up, till you also shall salute His sud-
den coming, and shall exclaim, Even so, come quickly,
Lord Jesus![29]

Appendix 4:

A Bibliography of the Pastor as Student

As FAR AS I KNOW, the following is the only attempt to construct such a bibliography for publication. It is not intended to be exhaustive, especially in the literature of the eighteenth century and in regard to pamphlet literature, which is extensive but generally not important. I have arranged the following in chronological order by date of first publication.

John Edwards (1637-1716). *The Preacher.* London, 1705. Vol. 1.

Cotton Mather (1663-1728). *The Student and Preacher.* London, 1781. Reprinted 1938.

James Mason. *Student and Pastor.* Exeter, 1794.

Edward Williams (1750-1813). *The Christian Preacher; or, Discourses on Preaching . . . with an Appendix on the Choice of Books.* London, 1800. 5th ed., 1843. "Catalogue of authors who may be beneficial to young preachers." This is a remarkable classification, often with extended remarks, of perhaps 1,800 titles, though so many of them are now forgotten, and some of them probably not to be found in any library in America.

George Pretyman Tomline (1750-1827). *Books for the Clergy.* 1799.

Edward Bickersteth (1786-1850). *The Christian Student.* London, 1829. 3d ed., 1832. 4th ed., 1844. Pp. xiv. 567 (about 2400 items).

Charles Bridges (1794-1869). *The Christian Ministry*. London, 1835. 6th ed., New York, 1847. Especially pp. 39-54.

Robert Turnbull (1809-77). *The Student Preacher*. 1854.

C. J. Middleditch. *A Minister's Books; or the Pursuit of Literature in Connection with the Work of the Ministry*. 1866.

Henry Ziegler. *The Preacher: His Relation to the Study and the Pulpit*. Philadelphia, 1876.

Charles H. Spurgeon (1834-92). *Commenting and Commentaries*. New York, 1876.

Austin Phelps (1820-90). *Men and Books*. New York, 1882.

John Shaw Banks (1835-1917). *A Preacher's Library: Hints on Theological Reading*. London, 1885. Rev. ed., 1902.

Robert W. Dale (1829-95). *Nine Lectures on Preaching*. Yale Lectures on Preaching 1877-78. London, 1890.

Samuel M. Jackson (1851-1912), ed. "A Ministerial Library." In *Theological Propaedeutic*, ed. Philip Schaff. New York, 1893. 7th ed., 1907. Pp. 53-596.

Charles E. Jefferson (1860-1937). *Quiet Hints to Growing Preachers in My Study*. 1901. Especially chap. 23. For the most part a bitter denunciation of those who, according to the author, read too many books.

Herrick, Johnson (1832-1913). "The Minister's Study." In *The Ideal Ministry*. 1908. Lecture 2.

Arthur S. Hoyt (1851-1923). *The Preacher: His Person, Message, and Method*. New York, 1909. Especially chaps. 4 and 5.

Anthony C. Deane (1870-1946). *In My Study*. London, 1913. A Roman Catholic.

George Jackson. *In a Preacher's Study*. London, 1914.

Anthony C. Deane (1870-1946). *A Library of Religion*. London, 1918. A Roman Catholic.

John A. Hutton (1868-1947). *That the Ministry Be Not Blamed*. New York, n.d. Lectures given in 1921. Especially pp. 148-74.

Stephen James Brown. *The Preacher's Library*. London, 1928. 14:129.

John W. Oman (1860-1936). *Concerning the Ministry.* New York, 1937. Especially pp. 114-29.

Herbert S. Box et al. *The Priest as a Student.* London, 1939. 14:380.

Wilbur M. Smith. *Profitable Bible Study.* Boston, 1939. 2d ed., 1963. "Basic Books for the Bible Student's Library," pp. 94-162.

Halford E. Luccock. *In the Minister's Workshop.* Nashville, 1944.

Elgin S. Moyer. *The Pastor and His Library.* Chicago, 1953.

Jay Smith. *Minister's Library Handbook.* Boston, 1958.

Mark W. Lee. *The Minister and His Ministry.* Grand Rapids, 1960. "The Minister and the Study," pp. 22-34, and "The Minister and the Books He Reads," pp. 253-75.

Notes

CHAPTER 1

1. G. Campbell Morgan, *Winona Echoes* (Winona Lake, Ind., 1919), p. 149.
2. John Henry Jowett, *The Preacher: His Life and Work* (New York: Harper, 1912), pp. 114-17.
3. Austin Phelps, *Men and Books* (New York: Scribner, 1891), pp. 315-20.
4. A. W. Dale, *The Life of R. W. Dale of Birmingham* (London: Hodder & Stoughton, 1898), p. 510.
5. Charles Guignebert, *Jesus,* History of Civilization (1935), p. 500.
6. Benjamin B. Warfield, *Revelation and Inspiration* (New York: Oxford U., 1927), pp. 229-50.
7. L. H. Grollenberg, *Atlas of the Bible* (London: Nelson, 1956), p. 139.
8. Ibid., p. 140.
9. *The Pictorial Biblical Encyclopedia* (New York: Macmillan, 1964), p. 456.
10. J. J. Von Allmen, ed., *A Companion to the Bible* (New York: Oxford U., 1958), p. 7.
11. Marjory Bonar, ed., *Andrew H. Bonar: Diary and Life* (New York, 1960), p. 168.

CHAPTER 2

1. Franz Delitzsch, *Prophecies of Isaiah* (London, 1880), 1:432-36.
2. John Calvin, *Isaiah* (Edinburgh, 1852), 1:184-85.
3. W. Robertson Nicoll, *Princes of the Church* (London, 1921), p. 85.
4. Ibid., p. 86.
5. G. F. Barbour, *The Life of Alexander Whyte*, 3d ed. (1924), pp. 289-90.
6. Robert S. Candlish, *The First Epistle of John Expounded in a Series of Lectures* (Edinburgh, 1866), pp. 546, 552.

CHAPTER 3

1. Andrew Martin Fairbairn, *Studies in the Life of Christ* (London, 1880), p. 1.
2. S. R. Driver, *Dictionary of National Biography Supplement* (London, 1901), 2:175-76.
3. Marcus Dods, Preface to *The Life and Times of Our Lord Jesus Christ* by John Peter Lange (Edinburgh, 1872).
4. *Westminster Theological Journal* 32 (Nov. 1969 - May 1970): 230.
5. Alexander Whyte, *The Walk, Conversation, and Character of Jesus Christ Our Lord* (1905), pp. 89-90.
6. Ibid., pp. 89-93.

7. From *Sketches* by Hazlitt, as quoted in *Anthology of Jesus*, ed. James Marchant, (New York: Harpers, 1926), p. 311.
8. William Arnold Stevens and Ernest DeWitt Burton, eds., *A Harmony of the Gospels for Historical Study* (1893), p. iv.
9. H. P. Liddon, *Sermons on Some Words of Christ* (London, 1892), p. 18.

CHAPTER 4

1. *The Cambridge History of the Bible*, vol. 1, *From the Beginning to Jerome* (New York: Cambridge U., 1970), p. 13. Used by permission of the publisher.
2. Ibid., p. 37.
3. Ibid., p. 237.
4. Ibid., p. 151.
5. Ibid., pp. 388-89.
6. Don Isaac Abravanel, *The Salvation of His Anointed* and *The Wells of Salvation*, as quoted by E. I. J. Rosenthal "The Study of the Bible in Medieval Judaism," in *The Cambridge History of the Bible*, vol. 2, *The West from the Fathers to the Reformation* (1969), p. 274.
7. Ibid.
8. As quoted in *The Cambridge History of the Bible* 1:547-48.
9. Ibid., p. 51.
10. Ibid., p. 159.
11. Ibid., pp. 475, 480, 485-87.
12. Ibid., p. 559.
13. Ibid., p. 434.
14. Ibid., 2:24.
15. Ibid., p. 282-83.
16. *The Cambridge History of the Bible*, vol. 3, *The West from the Reformation to the Present Day* (1963), pp. 316, 318.
17. Ibid., p. 333.
18. Ibid., p. 402.
19. Ibid., p. 383.
20. Ibid., pp. 507, 511.
21. Ibid., p. 519.
22. Ibid., p. ix.

CHAPTER 5

1. G. F. Barbour, *The Life of Alexander Whyte*, pp. 289-90.
2. G. H. Kurtz, *History of the Old Covenant* (New York, 1859), 1:44.
3. Wm. Hazlitt, ed. and trans., *The Table Talk of Martin Luther* (London: Bohn, 1857, pp. 4, 5.
4. Alexander Whyte, *Bible Characters: Our Lord's Characters*, p. 183.
5. John A. Scott, *We Would Know Jesus* (Chicago, 1936), pp. 124, 131.
6. Herrick Johnson, *The Ideal Ministry* (Chicago, 1908), pp. 143-44.
7. *Dewey Decimal Classification and Relative Index*, devised by Melvill Dewey, std. (15th) ed. rev. (New York: Forest Press, 1952).
8. Sir Martin Ryle, quoted by Yorick Blumenfeld, "Mapping the Vault of Heaven," *World*, September 12, 1972, p. 45.

APPENDIX 2

1. A. W. Greenup and J. H. Moulton, eds., *The New Testament in the Revised Version of 1881 with Fuller References* (Oxford: U. Press, 1910), p. ix.

APPENDIX 3

1. William Orme, The Practical Works of the Rev. Richard Baxter (London: James Duncan, 1830), 4:266-67.
2. Ibid., 5:584-85. Baxter's book list is on pp. 589-600.
3. Ibid., 2:151-52.
4. Charles Bridges, *The Christian Ministry*, from the 6th London ed. (New York, 1847), p. 49.
5. R. W. Dale, *Nine Lectures on Preaching*, 9th ed., (London: Hodder & Stoughton, 1896), p. 66.
6. Ibid., p. 69.
7. Ibid., p. 73.
8. John A. Hutton, *That the Ministry Be Not Blamed* (New York: Geo. H. Doran, n.d.), pp. 149-50.
9. Ibid., p. 152.
10. Ibid., p. 153.
11. Ibid., pp. 165-66.
12. Ibid., pp. 169-70.
13. H. C. G. Moule, *To My Younger Brethren* (London: Hodder & Stoughton, 1892), p. 60, n. 1.
14. W. Robertson Nicoll, *A Bookman's Letters* (London: Hodder & Stoughton, 1913), p. 229.
15. Ibid., pp. 231-32.
16. Ibid., p. 22.
17. Austin Phelps, *Men and Books* (New York: Scribner, 1891), p. 105.
18. Ibid., p. 132.
19. Ibid., p. 210.
20. Ibid., p. 220.
21. Charles H. Spurgeon, *Commenting and Commentaries* (New York: Sheldon, 1876), p. 62.
22. Ibid., p. 5.
23. Ibid., p. 11.
24. Ibid., p. 14.
25. L. Tyerman, *The Life and Times of the Rev. John Wesley, M.A.* (New York: Harper, 1872), 3:359.
26. L. Tyerman, *Life of the Rev. George Whitefield* (New York: Randolph, 1877), 2:583.
27. Alexander Whyte, *The Apostle Paul* (Cincinnati: Jennings & Graham, n.d.), pp. 16-17.
28. Ibid., pp. 19-20.
29. Ibid., p. 181.

Index

In this index, duplication has been avoided as far as possible. When the names of authors and editors are listed, the titles of their books will not be inserted. Thus the name of James Hastings appears here, but not the specific titles of the noted dictionaries which he edited. When titles of books do appear here, as the *International Standard Bible Encyclopaedia*, the names of editors will not generally be listed also. Some subjects discussed in this volume have been somewhat difficult to indicate in such an index as this, for example, the day-by-day experiences that so often threaten to interrupt those precious morning hours that have been set aside for study.

FREAKY
STORIES ABOUT
OUR BODIES

BY KRISTEN RAJCZAK

Gareth Stevens
PUBLISHING

Please visit our website, www.garethstevens.com. For a free color catalog of all our high-quality books, call toll free 1-800-542-2595 or fax 1-877-542-2596.

Library of Congress Cataloging-in-Publication Data

Rajczak, Kristen, author.
 Freaky stories about our bodies / Kristen Rajczak.
    pages cm — (Freaky true science)
 Includes bibliographical references and index.
 ISBN 978-1-4824-2960-2 (pbk.)
 ISBN 978-1-4824-2961-9 (6 pack)
 ISBN 978-1-4824-2962-6 (library binding)
 1. Medicine—Miscellanea—Juvenile literature. 2. Human body—Miscellanea—Juvenile literature. 3. Medical innovations—Juvenile literature. I. Title.
 R706.R35 2016
 610.2—dc23

                                        2015007002

First Edition

Published in 2016 by
Gareth Stevens Publishing
111 East 14th Street, Suite 349
New York, NY 10003

Copyright © 2016 Gareth Stevens Publishing

Designer: Sarah Liddell
Editor: Ryan Nagelhout

Photo credits: Cover, p. 1 (leg and arm used throughout book) Morphart Creation/ Shutterstock.com; cover, pp. 1 (fingernails), 7 (Chris Walton) STAN HONDA/Staff/AFP/ Getty Images; cover, background throughout book Graphic design/Shutterstock.com; pp. 5, 7, 9, 11, 13, 15, 17, 19, 21, 23, 25, 27, 29 (hand used throughout) Helena Ohman/ Shutterstock.com; pp. 5, 7, 9, 11, 13, 15, 17, 19, 21, 23, 25, 27, 29 (texture throughout) Alex Gontar/Shutterstock.com; p. 5 Boston Globe/Contributor/Boston Globe/Getty Images; p. 7 (normal cells) Onur Gunduz/Shutterstock.com; p. 7 (cancer cells) Lightspring/ Shutterstock.com; p. 7 (Chris Walton) STAN HONDA/Staff/AFP/Getty Images; p. 8 MedicalRF.com/Getty Images; p. 9 Scimat Scimat/Science Source/Getty Images; p. 11 Biophoto Associates -/Science Source/Getty Images; p. 12 Scewing/Wikimedia Commons; pp. 13, 24 Barcroft/Contributor/Barcroft Media/Getty Images; p. 15 (brain scan) Medical Body Scans/Science Source/Getty Images; p. 15 (nerves) Rallwel/ Shutterstock.com; p. 17 microgen/E+/Getty Images; p. 18 Arsgera/Shutterstock.com; p. 19 Harry Kikstra/Moment/Getty Images; p. 21 Bill Ingalls/NASA/Handout/ Getty Images News/Getty Images; p. 23 Materialscientist/Wikimedia Commons; p. 25 Getty Images/Handout/Getty Images News/Getty Images; p. 27 (Blade Runner) RubberBall Productions/Brand X Pictures/Getty Images; p. 27 (eye) Entheta/ Wikimedia Commons; p. 29 J. R. Eyerman/Contributor/The LIFE Picture Collection/ Getty Images.

Printed in the United States of America

CPSIA compliance information: Batch #CS15GS: For further information contact Gareth Stevens, New York, New York at 1-800-542-2595.

CONTENTS

Words in the glossary appear in **bold** type
the first time they are used in the text.

A NEW FACE

In 2008, a Texas man named Dallas Wiens was painting a building when an electrical wire hit his head. Wiens was burned terribly. He survived, but the skin **grafts** he received on his face healed to just bare flesh where his eyes and nose used to be. For years, Wiens lived with only a mouth opening. That is, until he got a face **transplant**.

The first successful organ transplant, a kidney, was performed in 1954. Since then, millions of people have received lungs, hearts, and many other organs. But it wasn't until 2005 that the first face transplant was attempted. Wiens's was the first full face transplant done in the United States.

There are lots of stories about the human body that are nearly unbelievable! Some are just freaky!

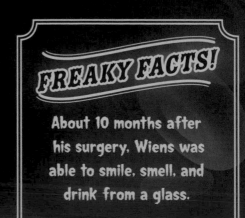

FREAKY FACTS!

About 10 months after his surgery, Wiens was able to smile, smell, and drink from a glass.

WIENS, SHOWN HERE, WAS BLINDED BY HIS ACCIDENT AND IS STILL UNABLE TO SEE.

WHOSE FACE WAS IT?

Many people are organ **donors**, but simply becoming one doesn't allow you to donate your face! The family of the person who died has to consent first. Once a face to be transplanted was secured for Wiens, more than 30 doctors, nurses, and others had to work for 15 hours to give him eyes, a nose, lips, and the needed muscles. Though Wiens received someone else's face, he didn't end up looking like that person. That would've been freaky!

5

YOUR UNUSUAL BODY

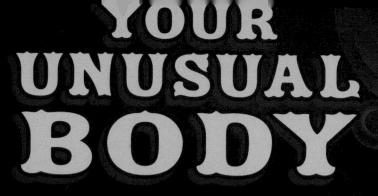

Many strange stories about the human body tell us about fascinating medical discoveries or disease. There are plenty of those in this book. But let's first look at some everyday functions and truths about your body. Some of it's pretty freaky!

The human body is made up of cells, which are the basic units of life. Yet millions of them die every day! Don't worry: they're supposed to do this. In fact, cells have a plan for their death inside them, just waiting for the signal.

While millions die each day, millions more are being created to replace them. Over the course of about 27 days, you'll **regenerate** the top layer of your skin. The lining of your stomach is replaced in about 3 days!

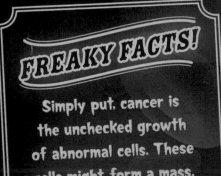

FREAKY FACTS!

Simply put, cancer is the unchecked growth of abnormal cells. These cells might form a mass, or tumor, and spread to other body parts.

WHEN NORMAL CELLS ARE CREATED, IF THEY HAVE DAMAGE, THEY'LL JUST DIE. CANCER CELLS CONTINUE TO CREATE MORE OF THEMSELVES, AS THE BOTTOM OF THIS IMAGE SHOWS.

HOW CANCER FORMS

NORMAL CELL

NORMAL CELL GROWTH

TUMORS BUD AND SPREAD THROUGHOUT THE BODY

MUTATION RESULTS IN CANCER CELL

CANCER CELL GROWTH FORMS TUMOR

EMBRACING THE WEIRD

Some freaky things about the human body happen naturally. For example, babies are born with almost 100 more bones than adults! Many of them are made of a soft tissue called cartilage and grow together into the 206-bone adult skeleton. Babies' kneecaps are just soft cartilage at first! Some people embrace the natural growth of the body a little too much. Chris Walton broke the world record for longest fingernails in 2012. The nails of her left hand grew to a total of 10 feet 2 inches (3.1 m)!

7

We're outnumbered in our own bodies! Even though your body has trillions of cells, there are about 10 times as many bacterial cells found in and on your body.

Did you know not all bacteria are harmful? While some kinds cause illness, other bacteria help your body work properly. Microorganisms, or microbes, live in your stomach and intestines to help your body break down food into **nutrients** it can use. Others make things the body needs and can't make itself, such as vitamins.

Some people's guts don't have the bacteria they need anymore. Doctors found a pretty freaky way to fix that: **fecal** microbiota transplants (FMTs). To many people—even those who might benefit from an FMT—this sounds too weird or gross to try.

FREAKY FACTS!

Among your body's bacteria are some pathogens, or the microorganisms that can make us sick. They only make you sick in certain conditions, though, and scientists are studying why that is.

COMMON STOMACH PATHOGEN, *HELICOBACTER PYLORI*

FMT

Not many doctors perform FMTs, though the number seems to be growing. In the United States, rules about studying human fecal matter for medical reasons are slowly changing as success from FMTs continues. FMTs have been especially successful for the treatment of an overpopulation of a harmful bacterium called *Clostridium difficile*, or *C. diff.* In an FMT, fecal matter from a donor is tested for the right good bacteria. It's then mixed with salt water, the solids are removed, and it's put into a patient.

CLOSTRIDIUM DIFFICILE

NOT HAVING THE RIGHT BACTERIA IN THE BODY IS OFTEN A RESULT OF TAKING TOO MANY ANTIBIOTICS, MEDICINES THAT FIGHT THE BACTERIA THAT CAUSE DISEASE.

A STRANGE GENE

Can you tell the difference between red and green? About 1 in 10 men can't! They're color-blind. Color blindness is one fairly common occurrence that's caused by a genetic mutation. No one knows you're color-blind unless you tell them, but some genetic mutations are easy to see.

Antonio Alfonseca was a relief pitcher in Major League Baseball from 1997 to 2007. He has a genetic mutation called polydactyly that caused him to develop a sixth finger before he was born! The finger is small and gave him no advantage when he pitched. Polydactyl people have six or more fingers or toes. It can be inherited, be part of a disease, or simply occur as a mutation on its own. Rarely, people are born with just one finger or toe. That's called monodactyly.

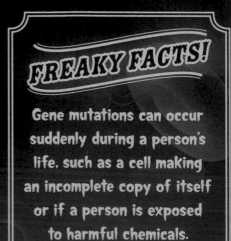

FREAKY FACTS!

Gene mutations can occur suddenly during a person's life, such as a cell making an incomplete copy of itself or if a person is exposed to harmful chemicals.

IT'S IN YOUR GENES!

Genetic mutations are changes to a person's **DNA** that make it
different from most other people's DNA. Some mutations are
inherited, or passed on from one or both parents. They include
hair color, eye color, and blood type. Inherited mutations may
also cause some disorders, such as albinism. People and animals
who have albinism don't make enough melanin in their bodies.
Melanin is the chemical that gives your hair, skin, and eyes color.

In 2011, another odd condition with a genetic connection made the news. The Guinness World Record committee named a girl from Thailand as the world's hairiest child. The girl, Supatra Sasuphan, was born with hypertrichosis, which causes excessive growth of hair on the body and face. Only about 50 cases of hypertrichosis, also called Ambras syndrome, have ever been recorded.

Scientists have found that some hypertrichosis runs in families, meaning it's a genetic mutation that can be passed on. Extra genes are found on a specific part of an affected person's DNA. These genes tell the body to keep growing hair.

Scientists might be able to create a drug that will act like the extra genes and turn on the hair growth gene. This discovery could help people with another genetic condition—baldness!

FREAKY FACTS!

People with hypertrichosis generally get rid of their body hair the same way other people do—cutting, shaving, or waxing. Some are treated with lasers!

SUPATRA HAS SAID SHE WAS TEASED AND BULLIED BY OTHER KIDS.

REAL WEREWOLVES?

The way hair grows on people with hypertrichosis may have helped start scary stories about werewolves being real! Today, hypertrichosis is even sometimes called "werewolf syndrome." However, we know now that hypertrichosis is inherited or can be caused by chemical imbalances in the body, not by a bite from a wolf during a full moon. Those with the syndrome can't help how their hair grows!

13

UNDER ATTACK

One of the major systems in the body is the immune system. Its job is to defend the body from germs, viruses, and other foreign matter. But what happens if the body thinks its own cells are the invaders?

Autoimmune diseases are those in which the body attacks healthy cells. That's downright scary! Sjögren's (SHOH-gruhnz) syndrome, for example, causes the body to attack and destroy the body parts that produce spit and tears, among other problems.

One of the worst autoimmune diseases is multiple sclerosis (MS). The immune system attacks the body's **nerve** coverings, making the brain unable to properly communicate with the body. In the worst cases, MS patients eventually can't walk without aid. People can live a long time with MS, but there's no cure.

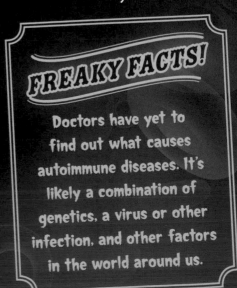

FREAKY FACTS!

Doctors have yet to find out what causes autoimmune diseases. It's likely a combination of genetics, a virus or other infection, and other factors in the world around us.

MS CAN OCCUR IN ANYONE, BUT USUALLY AFFECTS WHITE PEOPLE AGES 15 TO 60 WHO LIVE IN TEMPERATE CLIMATES.

WHAT IS IT, DOC?

Autoimmune diseases are some of the scariest things that can happen in your body. One big reason for this is it's very hard to diagnose autoimmune diseases. MS, for example, has many different symptoms, and not every patient has them all. There's also no one test a doctor can use to diagnose it. This is common among autoimmune diseases. People will often see many doctors and try many medicines before they're properly diagnosed.

15

TO THE EXTREMES

Your body can withstand diving into a few feet of water—and even belly flops. But SCUBA divers may dive down 100 feet (30.5 m) or more! The body starts to get freaky at that depth.

SCUBA divers breathe compressed air from a tank, which contains a small amount of nitrogen the body doesn't use. The deeper divers go, the more pressure there is on the **diver** and the air in the tank. As this pressure increases, more nitrogen **dissolves** in the body.

As the diver rises, the pressure becomes less, and the body begins to decompress. Surfacing must be done carefully because the dissolved nitrogen is released as bubbles. If the diver comes to the surface too rapidly, the bubbles build up, giving the diver decompression sickness, or the bends.

FREAKY FACTS!

A bottle of soda has bubbles in it, which is pressurized carbon dioxide. When the bottle is opened, bubbles rise to the top. That's what happens when a diver has nitrogen in their **tissues** and tries to surface too quickly!

FEELING THE DIVE

Divers who are diagnosed with the bends are very uncomfortable after their dive. They'll start having pain around their joints, especially their shoulders and elbows. Extreme tiredness and some difficulty breathing may occur. Sometimes divers go into shock. To prevent getting the bends, divers going very deep should slowly rise to the surface, stopping as they go to let the gas come out of their tissues a little at a time.

THE RISK OF THE BENDS INCREASES THE DEEPER A DIVER GOES.

Hundreds of people try to reach the top of Mount Everest every year. That means braving a terrifying area called the "death zone." It starts about 26,245 feet (8,000 m) above sea level. That's where oxygen in the air begins decreasing to levels that bother the body. Climbers have a hard time catching their breath, need more water than usual, and start to get headaches and feel dizzy. These are symptoms of altitude sickness, which is what happens to the body at great heights.

However, the human body can adapt. The body makes more red blood cells to better carry oxygen and starts to use more of its lung **capacity**.

FREAKY FACTS!

Periodic breathing, or periods of no breathing while asleep, is common when at high altitudes. Since we need to breathe to stay alive, that can be pretty freaky!

ALTITUDE DEATH

Before attempting the tallest mountains, climbers should climb smaller ones. This teaches their body how to adapt more quickly to higher altitudes. In addition, climbers should take weeks to climb huge mountains like Everest, stopping for days or weeks at the camps on the mountainsides in order to let their body adapt. Failing to do either of these things puts climbers at an even greater risk in the "death zone." Many have, in fact, died because of the altitude.

THE HIGHEST HEIGHTS

In March 2015, US astronaut Scott Kelly began a yearlong stretch aboard the International Space Station (ISS). Astronauts have been living aboard the ISS for more than a decade, and scientists have continually monitored how the human body responds to the journey, living in space, and coming home. There are still a lot of unanswered questions, and Scott and his twin brother Mark are hoping to help provide answers.

Mark Kelly, a retired astronaut, will undergo health tests while living his normal life on Earth. Mark's results will then be compared to his genetic copy Scott while he's living in space. They'll continue to be monitored when Scott returns to Earth after the year. The experiment is being called a once-in-a-space-program opportunity for scientists.

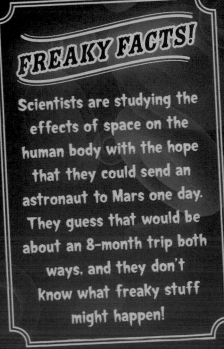

FREAKY FACTS!

Scientists are studying the effects of space on the human body with the hope that they could send an astronaut to Mars one day. They guess that would be about an 8-month trip both ways, and they don't know what freaky stuff might happen!

SINCE MARK HAS ALSO BEEN TO SPACE, THE EXPERIMENT ISN'T PERFECT—BUT SINCE SCOTT WILL HAVE BEEN IN SPACE ABOUT 10 TIMES LONGER THAN HIS TWIN, IT'S ABOUT AS CLOSE AS SCIENTISTS CAN EVER HOPE FOR.

SICK IN SPACE

Astronauts are able to adjust to zero gravity. However, about 40 percent throw up right when they reach space. That usually stops, but dizziness and a tired feeling may remain. In addition, astronauts have increased blood pressure, muscle loss, and likely many other problems that scientists don't know about yet! Everything about those living aboard the ISS is recorded for further study into how space affects the human body, including their bathroom habits!

21

BORN TOGETHER

On December 12, 2014, twins Carter and Conner Mirabel were born in Florida. These aren't just any twins, though. Carter and Conner are conjoined twins, born joined from the chest to the stomach. Conjoined twins are rare, occurring in only one out of every 200,000 births.

Carter and Conner had their first surgery just 3 days after their birth. In early January 2015, their small intestines were separated. Doctors found out during these surgeries that the boys had separate livers, but the organs had grown together. The doctors will wait until the boys are a little older to attempt separating them fully.

Separating conjoined twins is a difficult undertaking, but Carter and Conner are a type of conjoined twins called omphalopagus. This type of conjoined twins has had some of the most successful separation surgeries.

FREAKY FACTS!

Omphalopagus twins are those joined at the chest and stomach. About 33 percent of conjoined twins are omphalopagus.

HOW DOES IT HAPPEN?

Twins are two babies born at the same time. Identical twins come
from one egg that splits and two babies develop with the exact
same DNA. Conjoined twins also come from one fertilized egg,
but the dividing egg fails to fully separate. About 35 percent of
conjoined twins don't live longer than a day. The total survival
rate of conjoined twins is about 5 to 25 percent. Whether they
can be surgically separated depends on what organs and body
functions they share.

Krista and Tatiana Hogan were born in 2006, joined at the side of the head and part of their forehead. Amazingly, they were born healthy and stable, aside from their conjoined heads. Trying to separate two otherwise healthy little girls was a big risk, and their parents decided against it.

If conjoined twins are rare, those joined at the head, called craniopagus twins, are nearly impossible. Only about 2 percent of conjoined twins are craniopagus! But the Hogan girls are remarkable even among craniopagus twins: their brains are connected! Images of their brains show a piece of tissue one doctor believes connects one girl's thalamus to the other girl's thalamus. This means what Krista sees, Tatiana can name when she's blindfolded. When Tatiana drinks, Krista can feel it.

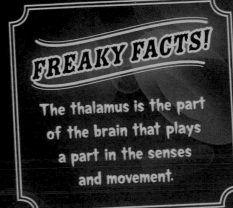

FREAKY FACTS!

The thalamus is the part of the brain that plays a part in the senses and movement.

JOINED SKULLS OF
CRANIOPAGUS TWINS

SEPARATE, BUT UNEQUAL

Some craniopagus twins must be separated. In the case of two
New York boys, Clarence and Carl Aguirre, doctors worried both
twins would die if they didn't act. Clarence and Carl shared a
part of their brain that had to be carefully divided. They were
2 years old when the tops of their heads were separated, and it
was mostly successful. Today, Clarence has few health problems,
but Carl has many health issues and likely permanent problems

PHANTOM LIMBS

Some people have parts of their body amputated, or removed, after a bad car accident or because of disease. Amputation is often a good thing. It may be done to stop an infection from spreading or to help a person recover from an accident more quickly. They might be able to do more activities over time than if they still had a crushed arm or leg that just wouldn't heal correctly.

But there's a truly freaky side to amputation—phantom limb syndrome. Amputees report feeling tingling, pain, heat or cold, and other odd sensations where their amputated body part once was. It's not certain why this happens, but some doctors think the brain is using the body's nerves to try to reconnect with the lost limb.

FREAKY FACTS!

The first reports of phantom limb syndrome came from a French surgeon in 1552. He wrote that soldiers with amputated limbs complained of pain in their missing arms and legs.

PROSTHETIC EYE

SCIENTISTS ARE WORKING ON MANY DIFFERENT KINDS OF PROSTHETICS. THERE ARE EVEN PROSTHETIC EYES!

PROSTHETICS

Many people around the world use prosthetics—or man-made replacement limbs—to walk and move more normally. A group called Amputee Blade Runners gives free running prosthetics to athletes who have lost a leg or were born without one. One of the group's founders, Ryan Fann, wanted to help change the lives of runners around the United States in the same way his was. Fann was given a prosthetic leg for running after high school and went on to run track at Tennessee State University!

DEEP FREEZE

As time goes on, some of the freaky things scientists have learned about our bodies won't seem so freaky anymore! However, even stranger stories may replace the ones in this book.

The growing field of cryogenics could bring about some of these oddities. Cryogenics is the study of what happens at very low temperatures. Freezing human blood and body tissue may become a common practice. Cryosurgery, or freezing parts of the body to destroy diseased body tissue, is already used to treat cancer and skin problems.

Some freaky stories about our bodies come from our ability to heal, and some of them arise from the amazing medical knowledge we have. What's clear in all these freaky stories is that the human body can withstand a great deal and still survive.

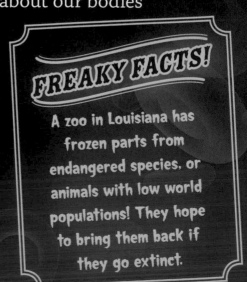

FREAKY FACTS!

A zoo in Louisiana has frozen parts from endangered species, or animals with low world populations! They hope to bring them back if they go extinct.

CRYONICS

In Clinton Township, Michigan, a building houses more than 100 dead bodies. These bodies float in huge tanks of nitrogen kept around −202°F (−130°C). Cryonics is the practice of freezing the human body after death, often with the goal of bringing it back to life once science knows how to cure certain diseases. Baseball player Ted Williams famously had his head frozen after he died. His family hopes he can one day be brought back to life.

29

GLOSSARY

capacity: the ability to hold or contain

diagnose: to identify a disease

dissolve: to mix completely into a liquid

DNA: molecules in the body that carry genetic information, which gives the instructions for life

donor: someone used as the source of body tissue

fecal: having to do with feces, or solid human waste

graft: a piece of human tissue attached to the body

nerve: a part of the body that carries messages between the brain and other parts of the body

nutrient: something a living thing needs to grow and stay alive

regenerate: to replace by a new growth of tissue

symptom: a sign that shows someone is sick

tissue: matter that forms the parts of living things

transplant: a medical procedure in which an organ is taken from one person and placed in or on another

FOR MORE INFORMATION

BOOKS

De la Bédoyère, Camilla. *Ripley's Believe It or Not: Human Body*. Broomall, PA: Mason Crest, 2011.

Perish, Patrick. *Disgusting Bodily Functions*. Minneapolis, MN: Bellwether Media, Inc., 2014.

Wilsdon, Christina, Patricia Daniels, and Jen Agresta. *Ultimate Body-pedia: An Amazing Inside-Out Tour of the Human Body*. Washington, DC: National Geographic Society, 2014.

WEBSITES

How the Body Works
kidshealth.org/kid/htbw/
Discover more about how the human body works here.

Organ Transplants
unos.org/docs/WEKNTK.pdf
Learn all about organ transplants from the United Network for Organ Sharing.

INDEX